UNDER A BILARI TREE I BORN

Bringing up nine children of your own is a major
achievement in itself. Bringing up a further 15
foster children is truly remarkable …

Alice Bilari Smith had lived in the Pilbara all her life, on
stations and in the bush, on government reserves and in
towns. As a girl on Rocklea Station she narrowly avoided
removal from her family by 'the Welfare'. Instead, Alice
learned to cook and launder, sew and clean; shoe horses,
chop wood and milk cows. Her working life on stations
continued as a young married woman and she added
mustering, dingo scalping, shearers' assistant and
sheep-yard building to her skills.

Alice Bilari Smith also grew up in the ways of her
country, hunting, cooking and building in the traditional
manner. Some of her children were born in the bush;
others in hospital. By the time she had five children of her
own she was playing an active role in caring for other
Aboriginal children and she initiated the establishment of
a Homemakers Centre in Roebourne.

Both a remarkable life and a typical life, Alice's story is
insightful and inspiring.

T0158594

Alice Bilari Smith was born at Rocklea Station in the Pilbara in 1923*, her mother being a Banyjima woman and her father a white teamster. She was raised by her Aboriginal family and, although she did not know it at the time, narrowly escaped being removed to Moore River. After marriage to Bulluru Jack Smith, Alice spent most of her adult years living in the bush and raising a large family. They retained their language and many of their customs, and it was not until 1969 that Alice settled in Roebourne so that her children could attend school. Living in Roebourne, she was a foster mother to fifteen children and a valued member of the community. Alice died on 1 February 2012 at Roebourne District Hospital.

Anna Vitenbergs was born in Scotland and came to live in the Pilbara where her father was wharfinger in the 1960s. For some years while her husband Robert was in the Royal Australian Navy they lived abroad or interstate, but were pleased to return to Point Samson with their family in the 1980s. They relocated to Denmark in the south of the state in 2012. Anna recorded the story and songs of Pilbara woman Lola Young in the book *Lola Young: medicine woman and teacher*, published in 2007 by Fremantle Press.

Loreen Brehaut is a New Zealander who lived in Western Australia for eight years while her husband Bill was working for Woodside Energy Ltd. While there she became active recording oral histories and was co-author of Florence Corrigan's autobiography, *Miles of Post and Wire*, which was shortlisted for the 1999 WA Premier's Book Awards.

Together Anna and Loreen collected the oral histories which developed into *The Kurrama Story*, and then recorded a major series of interviews about life in the Pilbara in pre-industrial days. This became the basis for the book *Pilbara Journey Through the Twentieth Century*.

* Here and throughout, words marked with an asterisk appear in Notes and Corrections on pages 234–35.

ALICE BILARI SMITH
WITH ANNA VITENBERGS
AND LOREEN BREHAUT

UNDER A BILARI TREE I BORN

Aboriginal and Torres Strait Islander readers are
respectfully advised that deceased people are
referenced in this publication.

 FREMANTLE PRESS

This edition published, with Notes and Corrections, 2015 by
FREMANTLE PRESS
25 Quarry Street, Fremantle
(PO Box 158, North Fremantle 6159)
Western Australia
www.fremantlepress.com.au

First published 2002 by Fremantle Press.

A project of the West Pilbara Oral History Group.

Consulting editor: Janet Blagg
Cover designer: Allyson Crimp
Cover photograph (aerial image): *Pilbara landscape* by Richard Woldendorp
Printed by 1010 Printing, China.

National Library of Australia
Cataloguing-in-Publication entry

Author: Smith, Alice, 1928–2012, author.
Title: Under a Bilari tree I born / Alice Bilari Smith, with Anna Vitenbergs
    and Loreen Brehaut.
Edition: 2nd edition
ISBN: 9781925162103 (paperback)
Subjects: Smith, Alice, 1928–2012
    Aboriginal Australians—Western Australia—Pilbara—Biography.
    Aboriginal Australians—Western Australia—Pilbara—Social life and customs.
    Aboriginal Australians—Western Australia—Pilbara—History.
Other Authors/Contributors: Brehaut, Loreen A., author. Vitenbergs, Anna, author.
Dewey Number: 305.8991509941

Fremantle Press is supported by the State Government through the
Department of Culture and the Arts.

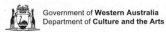

Publication of this title was assisted by the Commonwealth Government
through the Australia Council, its arts funding and advisory body.

For
my sons and daughters,
grandchildren, great-grandchildren
and cousin family

Alice Bilari Smith.

CONTENTS

AUTHORS' NOTE

This book was a true three-way collaboration. Alice had
met Anna and Loreen in conjunction with their recording
of Aboriginal oral histories and asked them to work on
her story. After several other projects were completed by
Anna and Loreen, the work began, assisted by a grant
celebrating the centenary of women's suffrage from the
Government of Western Australia. Alice and Anna met
regularly and twelve tapes of oral history were recorded.
These were transcribed by Loreen and organised into a
draft manuscript. Chapter by chapter, Loreen read this
version back to Alice for her comments and approval.
Changes, additions and deletions were made according
to Alice's wishes, and all three were satisfied with the
result. The project took over two years to complete and,
despite the difficulties presented by the fact that Alice
lived in Roebourne, Anna in Point Samson and Loreen in
Perth, they were proud of their joint effort and all
enjoyed the experience of working together and
becoming good friends.

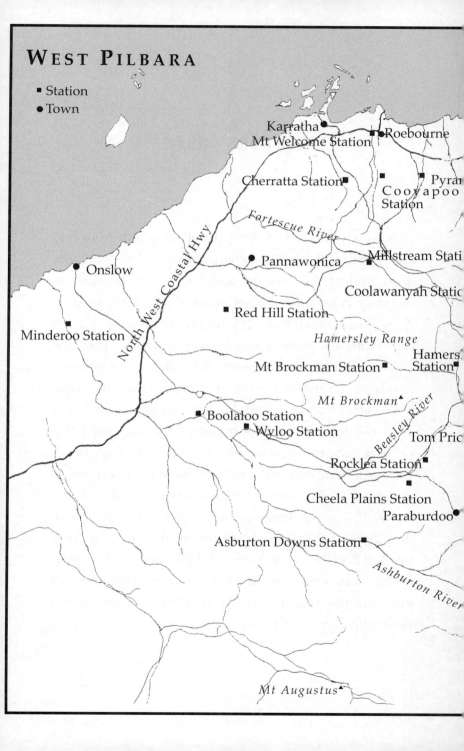

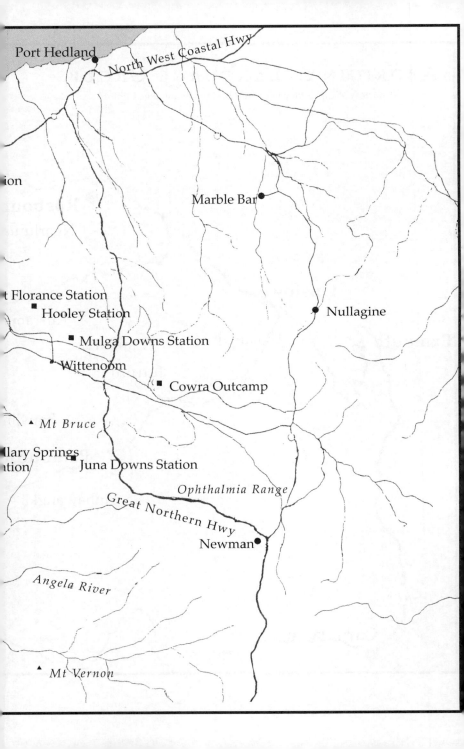

ABORIGINAL LANGUAGE GROUPS
(Courtesy Wangka Maya Pilbara Aboriginal Language Centre.)

Roebour

Ngarluma

Onslow

Kurrama

Exmouth

Thaiamyji

Pinikura

Jurruru

Banyjin

Paraburdo

Yinhawangka

Carnarvon

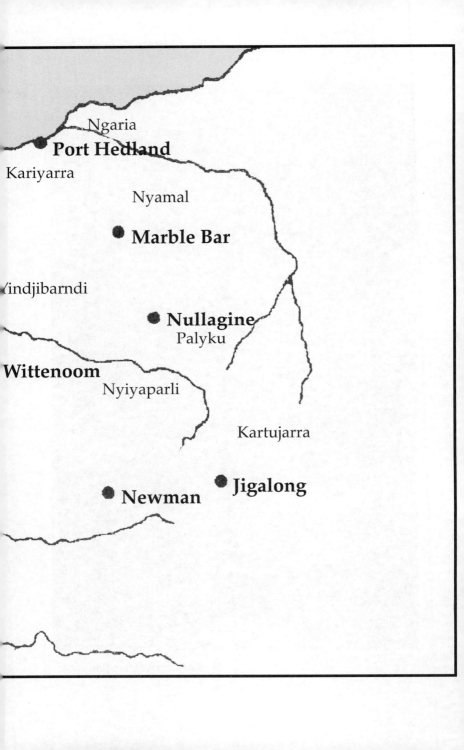

A bilari tree (Acacia atkinsiana).

1

BIRTH AND FAMILY:
COUNTRY AND STATION

Under a bilari tree I born, on Rocklea Station

I am Alice Smith, but my real name Bilari, because under a *bilari* tree I born, on Rocklea Station. I never had whitefella name, they used to call me Aborigine name: Bilari. Sometimes they say Bidayi; it's easier. Walter Smith wrote it down in his station book; the whitefellas used to have a record when we born. A few years ago we went to the museum in Perth, to see all the old papers, and when my daughter follow them history way back, from Rocklea Station, my name is there: Bilari, and I born 1928*.

We used to get fruit from that bilari tree, when they in season. He still standing too, that tree, but you can see we've been chopping it. He *big*, now! It's in Sandy Creek on Rocklea Station. Not only me — lots and lots of kids been born in that little gully.

My mother was a full-blood Aborigine; Banyjima

mother, Kurrama father. Her name was Yalluwarrayi, that's her Aborigine name, Yallu for short. Yalluwarri is the name of the windmill where she born. Maggie is her whitefella name. Her husband was George, and Yinba, that's his Aborigine name, he was my Aborigine stepfather. He had another name, too: Bindarngadi.

My whitefella father was old Alex Stewart. I could picture his face still, whitefella proper father mine. He used to drive a wagon with a camel team, coming up from Roebourne to take the food back to Rocklea. When the ship in Cossack, he used to come and get all the flour and things for every station up that way on the Top End. Then he come up the Big Hill on the old road from Roebourne. He do the contract, and if he have spare time, he work for Rocklea Station.

Alex Stewart was registered as an elector in the Pilbara district in 1929, and as a teamster on Pyramid Station.

Yinba, the one been married to my mother, and they been sharing a wife, those days. Before, they was fighting, Aborigine and the whitefellas, killing one another; that's the start-off. When they friends, that's what they done, sharing a wife now. My Aborigine father used to send my mother to go and get the tucker from my whitefella father, sleep with him and bring the food back in the morning, and that's how I come to be half-caste. They was both looking after me: I was a white kid, and my stepfather is a full-blood Aborigine; he was still looking after me.

My stepfather used to let me go with the whitefella

Camel team and truck meet, Mount Herbert (Big Hill).

father to camp one night along the road. We used to go with the camel team, chopping all the posts to build the shearing shed in Rocklea. We used to come to Turner River, near Wyloo, got all the timber and bring back to build the shearing shed. Yes, they both was looking after me: Aborigine father and a whitefella father. Alex Stewart had a white wife there too, and he had my stepsister and a brother. I only know the brother, Archie Stewart, but I forget my stepsister name. We all about the same age, we used to play together. Where that main stockyard in Rocklea now, that's where they used to be camping. They had a tent on the station. My father's wife accept me really good, and she used to tell me, 'That's your stepbrother and stepsister.' She didn't mind, she was good, too. We used to have a cake and a cup of tea, and she used to make all them Milo and things. She used to make a skirt and a blouse for us. She have that little sewing machine with the handle, early days one. She used to sew it with that. She was a nice lady, but she never been there very long, she had to went back to Sydney, because her two was schooling then.

So when they was about ten, eleven years old they went back to school, then; she wanted to keep them in the school in Sydney, and so I never heard anything more from them. She only come for a sort of Christmas holiday, and then they went back. Because too dangerous for the other Aborigine people; somewhere the wild Aborigines still around, so them two young one might be wander round, run into these people there. That's why they went back. We could have teach them how to work with the secret site and things, but the school was important to them. So mother take the two kids back to Sydney then. And then I think she died, and that's why we lose the boy and the girl then. That's what I heard from my dad, when he was alive. I never see them again. Even my father never heard anything from them again, when they went back, and he wasn't very long working then, my father, and he got sick. I still remember his face, because I was twelve years old when he died in Onslow, very old man. I think he went to hospital there. I still remember.

Sometimes you get bad people; not only whitefella

When the Aborigine and the whitefella first met up, they was fighting, kill one another. Sometimes you get bad people. Not only whitefella — we used to get bad Aborigine people coming from Meekatharra side. They used to come just like a big mob of army to spear them other lot Aborigine people in Turee and Rocklea, early in the morning before the sun come up. Not the Jurruru people that used to be there, and Pinikura people — they used to be good tribe. But the tribe from Mount Augusta, they used to be bad from there, they used to come early in the morning and kill all the people in here. They fight like soldiers, with them spears. They used to chase one another! You don't know when they coming. They used to spear the kids and all, same as the whitefellas. They kill the kids and wife and then all the man and boys.

Walter Smith and Len Smith, two whitefella brothers, they was single when they came looking for a station they could start somewhere. First thing they went to Bellary. They had only brush houses, made out of leaves, and the Aboriginal old people helped them to make a big boughshed. Later on they was building Rocklea Station. That was all Kurrama country.

Len Smith and Walter Smith had no white girlfriend, only Aborigine girlfriend. Walter Smith was the older one — he was about forty or fifty when he get there. He had a girlfriend, but he never had any family. Len Smith, the young one, been going around with the different wives. Jack Smith, my husband, was the first son Len Smith had. And then he found another woman and he got Clarrie Smith, another son. And the next son was Mundy* Smith — son of my sister, Annie Black. That was Len Smith's three sons.

Stations those days always had sheep, but no yards and no fences. The Aborigine people used to shepherd the sheep. They used to make a brush yard out of leaves, and they used to camp there, right round the yard, to save the sheep from the dingoes. My stepfather, when he was a boy, he start work for Len Smith and Walter Smith in Bellary Station. He was a mustering man, shepherding sheep, and my mother come there, married to her first husband, an old fella. Bellary was the station,

The three Smith brothers: Augustus, Frederick Walter and Oscar Leonard, went to the North-West in 1890, and worked as teamsters. Their father, Alfred Smith, also invested in the north, and was buried in Roebourne in 1897. The brothers formed a partnership and founded Rocklea Station in 1905. Augustus (Gus) Smith stayed on Pyramid Station near Roebourne, which he managed for the Meares family, while his brothers Walter and Len went up to the tableland country and ran Rocklea. Len Smith died in 1949 at the age of sixty-four, and is buried in Onslow cemetery. Walter's name was no longer on the Pilbara Electoral Roll after 1950. By then he was seventy-seven years old and, as Alice says, too old to run the station by himself. He seems to have left the district, but no definite record of his death has been discovered.

and Date Palm Spring was where they used to keep the sheep, because one side of the spring there is a steep hill, like a wall. They put brush around it and kept all the sheep in the corner, and they used to shepherd them out, feeding them.

My stepfather was a full-blood Aborigine, Kurrama man, and he used to be cattle mustering and sheep mustering, putting the shearing through. He was head stockman in the team, next to the overseer. One whitefella used to be overseer, running the big mustering team, but he was head stockman. And my mum used to drive the big spring-cart, moving all the stuff way out to the mustering camp.

And they all moved to the new station, now: Rocklea Station. Rocklea's the whitefella name, Jarrungka-Jarrungka is the Aborigine name. When they get Rocklea Station, they had three different breed horses. Wagon

PASTORAL PERSONALITIES—32

MR. FREDERICK WALTER SMITH.

The subject of our photograph this week is Mr. Fred. Smith,. a partner in "Rocklea" Station. This holding is situated on the Ashburton Watershed and slightly north of the Tropic of Capricorn. The country is of a very undulating nature, and within view of the station is the highest mountain in our State, viz., Mt. Bruce, 4024 feet. The climatic conditions are good and admirably suited for stock raising. The rainfall is fairly regular, and the average registrations range from 8 to 9 inches. The pastures are mainly plain

MR. FREDERICK WALTER SMITH.

and silver grass, salt bush and other edible shrubs, together with a fair area of mulga country. Water is readily obtained with large supplies at shallow depths.

The property carries approximately 16,000 sheep, a small herd of cattle and produces sufficient horses for the station requirements. The improvements of the holding include all the necessary homestead buildings, shearing and other sheds. Vegetables and fruit grow well and the supply of the former is ample throughout the year.

Dalgety's Review,
30 March 1933.

Rock engraving, Bellary Springs, near the old Bellary Station stockyards.

horses, the big draughty horse — big cart horse. And they had the stock horses to get the cattle, and they had the sheep horses. All the cattle horses, they used to put them in another paddock so they can breed there. And the sheep horses, they used to keep them near Rocklea, up by the Beasley River. Separate, because they got to have a stallion in it — the father of all the ponies. If they put them together, they'll be fighting. Everything was good. They used to go branding all the horses, and cattle branding. Yeah, he had cattle, and he had sheep, he had three lots of different breeds of horses in Rocklea. All around where Paraburdoo is now, and Tom Price, that's all horse country.

Walter Smith and Len Smith, they was special men. They know how to work with Aborigine people, and all the people come there from Hamersley and Brockman stations, because they had a bad man managing Brockman Station. He was Jimmy* Edney, and he was a cheeky man, always used the stockwhip on the men. They only had the fathers working in Brockman Station. The mothers and kids, they not allowed to be there, eat all the food — wife and kids got to go somewhere else. That's the sort of man he is. And that's how all the women come to Rocklea, from Brockman. We used to keep them in there. And old Roberts was in Hamersley Station — Bill Roberts — he's another cheeky one, too. They used to do the same in Mulga Downs Station — Johnny Hancock. He only want to keep all the men working, and don't want to feed the family. They used to be bad ones.

Only Len Smith and Walter Smith was a good person. And these two in Rocklea, they don't care how many family they had. They had *big* mob of people in Rocklea Station. One lot camping this side of the middle paddock, all Banyjima and Kurrama people — we had horse yard and the saddle room and things in the middle. And Yinhawangka other side of all the house and things there. Yindjibarndi people from Hamersley, they come and get mixed up with the Kurrama people; they start mixed up there. Big mob of people was there — I think might be two, three hundred Aborigine people. And they used to work, too, them old people, that's why Len Smith and Walter Smith liked them.

A big station, in the early days

Four different languages: Kurrama — they belong to the land there; and then my mob, Banyjima — my mum married towards the Kurrama. And then Yinhawangka people come from Turee, and they married towards the Kurrama ladies, and they settled down there looking after the mother-in-law and the father-in-law. And then Ngaria* people come; all the relations from Turee Station. Ngaria*, Yinhawangka, Kurrama and Banyjima — four tribe been there, marrying mix — they giving away daughter, because they're not allowed to just marry in the one family.

Rocklea Station comprised nine pastoral leases, totalling nearly 355,000 acres. It probably reached its productive peak in 1934: that year 28,600 sheep were shorn, giving a total of six hundred bales of wool. After that, successive years of drought resulted in diminishing returns; the wool clip declined each year until 1946, when there were only thirty-one bales. From 1936 until 1946 the Smith brothers applied for and were granted rent relief every year.

Yinhawangka people and Kurrama people only used Banyjima language then. They lost all the Kurrama and they lost all the Yinhawangka, the young generation kids like me. I had my own language all the time; Banyjima. They all using our language now. We used English as well, but just in the station with the Smith family, that's all.

We had four whitefellas at Rocklea. Walter Smith is the

Rocklea Station sheep yards, 1930s.
Stanley Delaporte's father's house is at the left rear.

Les Kempton carting Rocklea Station wool, stopped at Wyloo Station.

proper boss in the station and Len Smith is the manager, one overseer, and one — my father — is a camel team driver. One of the overseer we had — whitefella, Bedford Delaporte — he was a mechanic. He was Stanley Delaporte's real father. He's the one taught my husband fencing and sheep yard and the cattle yard and driving motor car and fixing motor car.

Those white people really understand about the Aborigine people, and understand our language, and the Aborigine people really got a respect to them whitefellas. They used to be really friend, no fighting or anything. Whatever job the boss tell them to do, all the Aborigine people they do it properly. Not like this time — they do a little bit and go leave the job. But those days they got to finish that job properly. They had a lot of cattle and a lot of sheep and horses. That was a big station, in the early days. The windmills still there — I know all them names, the windmills' name. I've been grow up in Rocklea Station.

Those days there's lot of Aborigine people out in their own country. All the grannies and grandfathers — very old people. They don't want to leave their home — they stay there. And the people from the stations, they used to bring the food for them: bit of flour and tea and sugar, when they go on holiday. They used to take them to the old grandmothers and uncles and aunties. White people never used to have anything to do with them. Len Smith and Walter Smith, they don't interfere with the old people, where they want to live. That's their area, they

Buminha Spring*, where Bumah (Dinah) was born.

love to stay there till they die. Some old people used to be in the station, Walter Smith and Len Smith used to look after them, give them rations all the time. Every Sunday we used to get food for the old people: flour and tea and sugar and things; tobacco. Used to be stick tobacco those days, them square ones.

My mother, Maggie, she used to drive the big spring-cart, take all the swags and food and things, forty-four gallon drum, all the things in the back of that spring-cart. Got all the food, tuckerbox, swags, everything, wherever they going to make a big camp, and then she do all the cooking. Only men come out unload all the heavy things, and she used to cook — make damper, bread, whatever they want. She had one of my aunty to help: Dinah is the whitefella name, Bumah is the Aborigine name, because she born in Buminha* Spring, not far from Tom Price.

My mum carried the babies with her. When she cooking, she put them in the blanket on the ground. She put it there when she start cooking and carting water or whatever. We used to have them cyclone bed, but they never used to leave the baby on the bed, because the baby might roll over when she go get the water. Make a bed on the ground and the baby'll be laying on the ground asleep, and she go looking for wood and all. They used to have the baby with them all the time. If it's a real baby that couldn't sit up or anything, well they had a special yandy dish — wooden one, carry it under the arm. If he's asleep, leave him in that little yandy dish, and put a rock each side to hold it so it don't roll over. And the baby sleeps till he wake up self, while the mother do the jobs. Might be cooking or making fire or carting water.

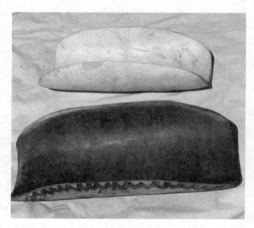

Yandy dishes for carrying babies. Made by Peter Stevens.

2

CHILDHOOD ON ROCKLEA STATION

We learnt more of the Aborigine way
than the whitefella way

My stepfather George had three wife, but one had no children with him. Inga worked as a stockman* — that's Stanley Delaporte's mother, she had Stanley before she come to my father. Then my Aunty Dinah, and my mother. We only had three kid belong to my stepfather. My aunty had one, Merru George, and my mother had two: my sister Jessie and me. We all brought up brothers and sisters. Even Stanley Delaporte, he was a stepbrother belong to us, because his mum been married to my stepfather. We was all together — he used to look after all the kids, my stepfather. Even my oldest brother and sister, they used to still come to my father, because the mum there. Those days we used to be one family all the time. Every family like that. They never say, 'You not belong to here.' They used to look after one another all the time. He look after all the kids and the wife from dangers. Doesn't matter about whose kid, because they're all their family.

Good man used to be a good husband, to look after the wife. Before the mum and dad give away their daughter, they look at the mother and father of that man, how they been keep their family, and how they been married, looking after their kids. They know the bad ones, they don't get mixed up with them sort of people, they got to go for the people that got good family.

Wives don't get jealous of one another, they just live together. They used to work different jobs. When one was free, when the husband gone, they might be got a boyfriend behind them; all them sort of thing they work out. Boyfriend behind the back! That's what they used to do. When the husband find out, they have a fight then, and when they have a fight, that boyfriend and girlfriend won't be meeting one another no more, they finished then. No children used to be, those days, I don't know how, with all the different father. I never seen one. They must have been careful!

We used to live not far from the homestead. Just some tin house — old people used to make it — and the boughshed with the fresh leaf. We used to make a boughshed with a fork tree — brush houses. We used to cover them up, and we'd make a little door that we can close in wintertime. Summertime we keep it open. On the top, you put the leaf first inside, and then put spinifex on the top, then put paperbark bark on the top like a tent. And you got to have a little roof, cover it up with leaves on the top to hold it down. Then no rain will get through.

They just used an axe, no saw. Chopping big wood with the axe, but those days those old people was really strong; they used to it, they been working like that all their life. They used paperbark tree for the building, so the nails can go in. Some wood is hard.

We used to have them cyclone beds — the hard one, iron one, and some old people used to make a wooden one. Get a fork stick and make a bed, get all the rail together till it turn into bed, then we used to put spinifex on the top. We used to get a sheepskin — been sheared, no wool — and we used to sit that on top. We used to tan that skin first to kill the smell and make it like leather. Then we used to use it to cover the spinifex on the top of the bed. When we were shearing, we used to get the old pieces, fill an old bag, take them down to the tub and wash it all clean, and then make some sort of cover, and we have a mattress then. And the pillow, we used to make it out of the sheep wool. We had blankets on the station in wintertime. The boss used to get a lot of blankets and sheets. But when we was in the bush, before the blanket come, we used to use the paperbark tree from the river. Summertime is hot — we used to sleep outside all the time. Station people never worry about cold air-conditioning or something. We used to have the summertime, we used to have the wintertime; we know how to manage.

On the floor we put clean sand from the river. We used to make a broom out of tea-tree, but we call him *gulimba* tree; leaf all skinny. We used to tie them up and sweep all the ground with that. Swept round the camp and swept round the fireplace. If there's any bones we put it all in heap and burn it up. That's what we used to do.

We used to get our water from the river. If there's a big pool, we dig a soak, because that's got green stuff in the pool, algae. We make a soak a long way from the pool, and clean it with a cup — nice and clean. Nice rainwater all the time — clear water. We used to carry it on the head in tin buckets, the square kerosene tins. We used to wash that clean and keep it for the water carting. And sometimes we got a proper steel bucket. We used to cart water to a little tank they used to have with a tap on the bottom of it. Fill that up and put a lid on and keep it clean. Everybody worked the same. No one had a different job. At the Rocklea homestead, they had a pipe there, and rainwater tank and everything, but they never run the pipe to the Aborigine camp. We used to cart water from there to our place, where we lived.

We did the washing in the homestead, because all the taps were there, big ones, and the copper to boil the clothes clean. Everybody used that. Sometimes some of the other people went to the overseer's house, and he had everything there for washing, too, because we were too many people to do all the washing in one place.

There was a blacksmith shop where they did the horseshoes, spring-cart wheels and things like that. He had a bathroom near that where the working people

Old Rocklea Station showing the kitchen, dining room and office.

would go have a bath, because there was a tank on top of a big stand, and you got cool water all the time. That's why we had that bathroom there. Everybody used the shower near the homestead in summertime, and wintertime we made hot water in a bucket and had it in the bathtub. A cement floor, and water going down to the river. And sometime we used to wash the clothes from the body, clean it there and come back clean, wet!

We had a dry toilet in the station. When he get overfull they used to burn it all up. Put a fire down the hole and get it clean. It used to be big tank, and on the top of the tank is the toilet seat there. They used to lift that up when they want to burn the thing, and they used to paint it with tar inside, keep it nice smell. It was good.

We used to get a haircut from one of the old ladies. We had a big comb, no brush. If we tangled up, they used to cut it short so we can put the comb through. Men too, they used to have a haircut from one lady. Sometimes we had head lice. We call that *gurlu*. We had that, but the old people used to clean it all the time, picking with the hand, you know, pull them all out. And we used to get a little comb, short one, and get all the gurlu out then, killing all the eggs.

My mum and dad had to look after me, or grandmother, if your mother's mum was alive. But I had no grandmother, only had Mum and Dad and my aunty. Whatever people in that camp, they look after the kids there. If we got an old lady, we got to keep that old lady, look after that old lady too. And if somebody's going out — hunting, maybe — someone's got to be home to look after the kids and the old ladies. Because if any danger comes, they know they've got someone there.

If I stay with somebody else and if I naughty girl, they got to give me a hiding, and when my mother find out I got a hiding from that one, she say, 'Good job!' Yeah, I'm going to get another hiding from her! Even the grown-up man, young son belong to my mother, if he makes trouble, he gets speared in the leg, and when he comes limping over there to my mother, she'll give him a hiding then. That's what he wants, see. And little children know when they go to play with other children, if they get naughty now, they know that old lady sitting there is going to do something, hit them. And next time they'll be good.

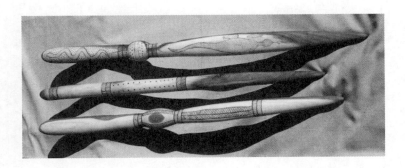

Digging sticks, used for digging up yams and other roots.
Made by Peter Stevens.

When I was a little girl, they used to get material, and one of the ladies used to make the clothes. When my proper father's wife had gone, one of my cousins was an old lady, and she had the sewing machine then. Same sort, a winding one, and she used to make the clothes for us. And then we learned, Walter Smith teach us, when I was eight or nine years old. Needle and cotton, sew it with the hand, and we used to make our own dresses then.

No shoes. In the middle of the day out on the flat it was hot, but we couldn't feel it; the bottom of our feet were hard just like shoes. Like a camel, hard, you couldn't feel it. We could walk all day like that. But when I came to town life, I couldn't walk like that any more — it's hot! We had no shoes — all the kids grew up like that.

Every Sunday we'd go hunting bush tucker. From Monday to Friday we stayed in the station, having the whitefella food, and when the Saturday came, we took off bush, camping; living on the wild food now. Getting the wild potatoes and the wild onions, and the kangaroo and the wild honey, all them things. Cooking it out in the bush. Wintertime we used to look for *kukutarri**. It's got a pink flower, and it's like a carrot, but it's a really soft one, and you cook it, it's nice — a sweet one! Sunday we'd start coming back, we had a lot of food in the spring-cart, then; we'd bring it back for the old people, specially the grandmothers. We had to work on Monday. We used to fill a bag to bring them home and give to the old people. And we used to bring the cooked kangaroos. We used to look after the old people; they couldn't move around. We used to bring them something, and we used to wash their clothes.

We only played with sticks and rocks — that's all we used to play with. We might make a yard with all the rocks, and make a little bit of island or something. That's all we used to do. We never used to play motor car and things, because we didn't know motor cars. When I was a kid I never used to see motor cars, only horses and carts those days. We used to get a stick like a spear, then put a bridle on the head part with some sort of string, then run around with that, chasing one another. We ride that one, and we used to gallop — but by running, not the stick!

We used to play fighting, too. We used to get little waddies. All the girls would fight with the waddy, and all the boys with the spear — blunt one, you know, not a sharp spear. Little spears they used to make. Sometimes they used to spear us! We used to guard it with the waddy! We used to play that one, but they used to blunt that thing first, then it was all right. It was good training for the boys, even to throw the boomerang. Proper big boomerang, you know; they used to take us to the flat to watch them throwing the boomerang, and they used to teach all the boys to throw the boomerang. That's all we used to do; nothing else than hunting, look for kangaroo, or digging goanna in the hole — all them things.

We never been to school. All we got was English words from the old people that looked after the station boss. That's where we got the whitefella language. And he taught us the whitefella's way, how to work, that's another good thing he done. They liked work — because they was building a new station, see. But we learnt more of the Aborigine way than the whitefella way. No station school, nothing. All the stations: Mulga Downs, Coolawanyah, Mount Florance, and Hooley and Rocklea, Turee and Mount Vernon, had no school. Ashburton, Wyloo — nothing. I been all around those stations — no schooling. They used to teach their own children with the radio work, but just for the white kids. Coolawanyah was doing it. They never asked all the Aborigine people, they just do it for white blokes. All of us — whatever people were there in the 1930s and 1940s, we've never been to school.

We used to be funny ... all the little girls

We used to be funny when we was little. All the little girls went together — we liked staying in the homestead with the old fella, Walter Smith. We used to tease him. He'd be sitting writing, we'd go peeping, watching him. And we'd throw a rock and things, you know, in the room, and when he came out looking, we'd run to the little gully there, behind the cook room. And when he found out, he used to smack us with a bag or something, and in the morning he'd give us a good work; dig the ground for the plant. That was okay by the mother and father because Mum and Dad know what we doing — they know we're teasing old fella. Because he was old man, you know, proper middle-age.

We used to have a big nice garden there, grapes and everything growing, and he had a barbed-wire fence round. He used to tell us to go and feed the chooks and get the eggs — every three o'clock. Oh, big mob of girls happy, going up. We pick up a piece of wire, we go looking. 'Oh, grapes here!' We go for the purple one. We'd tie the barb back — night-time we're going to come there. We'd tell a lie that we're going to have a bath to cool down in the big trough there. Then we're thieving, jumping through there — we holding the wire, get all the grapes, put them all inside our clothes and run away and have a feed then! But that old fella, he knew all those footprints there! He'd aways go to the garden in the morning; eight o'clock he'd go to the garden. He'd look around, look around, 'Oh, there's Alice Smith, there's Hilda, there's Dora Gilba.' All right — he knew now how many people have been in that garden.

When he came back, he'd tell us. 'Right — get the horse tail, now, and get the brace! You lot have been stealing my garden — you've got to work, now! You've got to work on that horse tail, plaiting it.' They used to cut the horses' tails for the saddles. We had to plait it, and after, we had to roll it back. We got a bucket boiling, and when we'd finished we had to put them all on to boil — they get soft then. When it's ready, we'd get all the tails with a wire hook, put them on the bed, let them get dry, and tip the hot water out. Next morning, get up, same job. We had to get it ready for the saddle. One white-

Leary Delaporte, 1995,
who grew up on Rocklea Station.

fella, Jack Edney, used to be a saddling man; he'd come and do all the saddles, and we had to get that horsehair ready for that man to sew the saddles. That's the punishment. We think we could fool him, you know, that he couldn't remember all our footsteps, but he know all the footprints, because we grew up with that man all the time!

We just wander round and play most of the time, all the young girls. We used to be nine girls: Hilda, Leary, Dulcie, Trixie, Mabel, me, Amy, Joyce and Dora Gilba, all of us together going round like that. Sometime we used to have a fight — big fight — just the girls. Something up, and we *big* fight, and start all the mothers fight, then! Just fight for a little while and come back good again.

We used to go everywhere in the bush. We go hunting wild beans, put them all in a dish, bring them back to the old people, and we cook it all up and peel it up, put all the seed and let the old people have it. Always something to do. Soon as you get up the morning you got some things to do.

Lot of young boys was there, too. Jack Smith, and Mitchell Cox, Bill Cox, Jumbo Giggles — Amy's brother — and Injie, and Limerick, and Arthur Cox, and Gilbert, and Thomas, and David. And Chubby Jones, eleven. Big mob boys, but they not allowed to come near the girls, you know. Daytime we could play together, but when late, they got to be separate.

Soon as after six o'clock, all the boys got a man there

Nelson Hughes, Jumbo Giggles and Peter Stevens, 1995.

looking after them, middle-age man, don't get mixed up
with the girls. And girls got special middle-age woman to
look after them — they got to be separate, those days. We
play one side and the boys play one side. If we still want
to play, right up to eight o'clock or nine o'clock in the
night, well we got someone there look after us all the
time. When nine o'clock come, well we go back home
now. I go back to my mum, and other lot go back to
their mum.

The boys about thirteen years old, they got to stay with
that man, but the girls thirteen, they got to go back to the
mum. That's the way we used to. And no more moving
like here — they still go around at eleven o'clock or
twelve o'clock in the night, in the street. But in the station
we had our different lives. Half-past five, six, the boys go
separated with the men, and the girls go separated with
the womans; now — they gone. All the time now, they

watch, till they go to bed. They don't let them go mix up, boyfriend and girlfriend, because those days not allowed young people have a girlfriend. They got to wait till given away to different tribe; not allowed to be one family. They used to watch.

Every fortnight they used to go for the mail, and a carton of apples always came. They used to bring bananas from Carnarvon. One of the whitefella friends of Walter Smith, the boss for Kooline Station, Peter Joy, he used to bring two cartons all the time to Rocklea Station, and that's only time we used to have bananas. We never had a banana tree there. Only those two fruit we used to get from outside: banana and apple. Orange and everything else we had growing there.

We had a big garden there. We had everything: cauliflower, turnips, beetroot, cabbage, carrots and parsnip. Chilli — them round hot one, we had that — and capsicum. Fruit — grapes, lemon and orange trees, and fig tree. We had five of them big ones. The old people used to be camped there in the garden all the time, watching for kids stealing! Yeah, we fellas! The middle-aged ones used to camp there, under the tree. They used to look after the garden because they know the young people's all going pinching things. They'd be weeding and gardening, and pinching the people like me. They're the one got to look after the garden during the day or night. But we used to sneak in other side!

The old people, when there was too much of

something, like figs, they used to open them up and leave them to dry on the top of the boughshed, let them get dry properly. When they're really hard then they put them in a bag — a clean white flour bag. Then when they go on holiday they've got a lot of food going out. Even the sugar or tea, whatever is any left over, they fill one of the bags. That's for the holiday, saving that. You see flour — two, three bags; sugar — two bags; tea — two bags. When they go on holiday they've got everything ready. They'd go for a long time; two, three months before they can come back again. They used to be clever, them old people.

Every wintertime we'd strip out the old plants, cut the ground, and put all the new ones in again. We had the sheep manure all the time, that's all we had: sheep and the cow. In the summertime, watermelon, rockmelon, pumpkin. We used to have *big* pumpkins — them orange ones. They grow really hard, and you have to chop it with a chopper. When I was a girl, there used to be lot in Rocklea.

When I was eight, I understand about all the work I do. My mum would tell me, 'Help this one, help the old people, or help somebody with two or three kids,' like that. 'Go and help them, look after their kids,' you know, while the mum doing something, until the mum finish the job, and then I go play round then. Sometime I go get water for the old people, go to the tank and get a billycan of water or something, bring it back to them. They chew tobacco, you know, mixed with ashes; we cook that one.

We go get some snakewood, might be one mile away from the camp, bring it back, burn it, put it all in a tin, and give the old people that one, let them keep it in the tin.

In that camp, they teach us look after the grannies. Bake a damper or cook meat or boil the billy — all them things. We had no stove then; we had camp fire all the time. Make a damper in the ashes, and boil the food. Sometimes we cook it in the frying pan, because we had a frying pan, when I was a kid. They used to cart all the wood to the homestead, so old people and everybody got to get wood from there. We used to cart wood for all the grannies, and the boys used to cart all the wood for the old grandfathers. Maybe this fella lose his wife, and this old lady might lose her husband, but we got to look after them, all the young girls.

We used to like it, too. Young girls, they think themself big. We used to go get the ration for the old people every Sunday, from the store: flour, tea, sugar, some stick tobacco. Get that, and a box of matches, and soap to wash your face. Baking powder. We take them back to the old grannies, and they used to tell us, 'You ones want to make a *marrimirri**' — that's what they call damper, *marrimirri** — 'we hungry.' We cook them up damper, we cook up meat. Sometimes they say, 'Cook it in the coal,' because old people like it like that, not in the frying pan, just on top of the coal; we used to cook it like that for them.

Mostly we used to kill a sheep. We used to have a killer in the pen all the time, and whenever we ran out of meat we used to get the butcher to go and butcher it and cut it up. The old people used to get all the tummy, and the head. We used to cook the head in the ashes, make a round hole, and make a fire there, and them old people waiting. Nice, too; I like it like that, sheep head. They just put it in the flame first, get all the wool out, then check the horn, and put it in that hole, now, bury it with the hot coal. When you bring it up, it's nice. Even the bullock head, the old people used to do that. But sheep head, you can cook it easy, because it's little. The old people used to like it. When I was a girl I see all that thing happening like that. I don't know where those old people learnt to cook that, because sheep, he doesn't belong to the Aborigine people. I don't know how they got it! Probably early days whitefellas, I think they're the ones who teach them how to cook the heads. A lot of whitefellas used to be hunting gold, and they used to get a sheep.

Nobody used to have accidents, nobody used to be sick. We only lost one, Dora Gilba's mum, and the baby, but I don't know what trouble they had. Dora Gilba's my little cousin-sister. The mother died and the baby died, both of them. We was living in the station then. Nobody been drowned. They used to watch the kids — nobody was allowed to go to the water without the big people. We used to swim in the running water; they used to teach us how to cross the river. They used to watch out where they've got to cross it, in the slow water. They used to put the little people on the back, and some little people might be held in the arms, and they swimming across the river. Nobody used to be drowned. I never heard of it anywhere, even in the Ashburton. The Ashburton people used to be clever, too: they used to cross that big river.

No measles, no chickenpox, no any of the sickening, we used to have. Disease. We used to get colds a little bit, or cough, but we used to have bush medicine all the time. And the witchdoctor, that's what we had.

3

STAYING WITH THE WHITEFELLAS

I don't follow them, because I used to be scared

When I was ten years old, my stepfather died — they strangled him, another lot of Aborigine people. Those days was really bad. They wanted the wives from him. His own brother, too — Dora Gilba's father — he went against him too. He wanted his other wife Dinah, my aunty. The wives didn't know they were going to do that. They was going round behind the back of my stepfather, you know, they was girlfriend and boyfriend about a year. And those men couldn't fight my stepfather, because he can fight, see, in the spear, boomerang and things. He was a good fighter in the spear, so they had to strangle him in the dancing time; night-time — bush dance, with the men. They had to do it secret way. They had a bush dance, without the women — the men's one. Just tell lies. That's when they strangle him there. I was only ten years old then. I know it still.

About a couple of weeks after, the wives just move in to the other husband, even my mum. She just have to go,

47

Yinba's (George) burial site on Rocklea Station.
The plaque reads: 'Burial site. Please respect. To damage or alter this site in
any way is an offence. Aboriginal Heritage Act'.

because other way she going to get killed. That's the way they work, see. Those days — early days — it's different; she have to go whether she like it or not. When I find out my stepfather get murdered, and that's that murder man that marrying my mum, then I just didn't wanted to go with them all the time. Wherever they go, I don't follow them, because I used to be scared. I used to stay in the station all the time with the whitefellas, with Len Smith and Walter Smith. I grow up just with the whitefellas in the station.

They don't report to the police, they just keep it to themself. He had a proper burial. They never got in trouble, all of them, but something went against them — they're all dead now. Because a lot of people from the other side of Turee, right back to Turee Station, they was crying for him, because he was a Law man. Proper Law man, and they just killed people one at a time, then, in the bush way, and they all died, all of them. They used to be really bad, those days.

He didn't make us work, we just worked for him

I was ten years old then, when Walter Smith started teaching us. We were always in the house, in the homestead. We want lolly. We was willing to do anything for him. We started off feeding the chooks. Chooks used to be about half a mile from the homestead. And then we used to go and feed the sheep — the killer we used to have in the yard. We used to go and feed that one, put water and everything, make sure they okay. Then we come back to do a bit of sweeping round the house, outside.

And then when we was turning twelve he tell us to start watching him cooking everything, baking in the oven. We started like that, baking things. He didn't make us work, we just worked for him. Then he started giving more jobs then; we keep going now. Teach us more and more. He used to chop all the meat in the butcher's shop, and he used to fill that baking dish, and we had to go and put it in the cooler. We used to do all them things for him. He used to tell us to go and get vegies — might be cabbage or cauliflower or whatever he needed to cook. We used to go and get it and he used to tell us to chop it up and put it in a pot, cook it.

You might go to the homestead and first it might be wood-chopping time; chop the wood, fill the wood box. We used to use the axe, chop all the wood in the wood heap. If the men were too busy, well we have to chop it, the girls. Sometimes middle-aged womans chop it, and we used to cart it in the wheelbarrow to the homestead. Fill the wood box in the wall outside, to use it for cooking. We had a big wood stove, two-door, so we can fit everything in there, roasting meat or baking bread. We used to bake six bread every day, big loaves of bread in a long tin. We used to bake that with yeast — we used to make it in a bottle all the time. Nice bread, they used to make. Sometime we made a damper, baked it in the oven.

Len Smith and Walter Smith taught us how to cook whitefella way, and waitering job, and sweeping floor with a broom, and baking bread and cooking roast in the oven. How to go and butcher the sheep, and washing up dishes. My mother was started like that, then when we got big enough we used to do the same.

We used to milk the cow every morning, and boil the milk. And we separate the milk from the butter, and we saved the milk in the cooler. There was a big cooler at the homestead, the sort with flywire around it, and a big shallow dish full of water on the top and he overflowing all the time on to the cloths hanging down all round. Keep it cool, all the meats and things, nice. Butter and things wouldn't go bad. We used to wash it inside all the time, keep it clean, put the new lot of stuff there. Might be four shelves that all the different foods got to be on. Meat in there, and whatever vegies you've got for use, from the garden.

Some of the older ladies, they were there too, teaching us. We used to make the soap ourselves — washing soap — from fat. The boss showed them how to do that, and now we used to watch them doing it, all the old ladies. We used to melt the fat — sheep fat, rendered — and put it all in a big tub, like a big bathtub, but specially for the soap. Let it get a little bit cooled down. We mixed caustic soda in water, half a four-gallon bucket, mixed it with the melted sheep fat, and we had to stir it up till it got hard like custard. We leave it for a night then. In the morning we come back, and this big thing's set now. We had a table with a wire in the middle, and a rail, and we cut it all in slices — long ones first, and then we turned it around and cut it in little blocks. We used to make about forty in that one tub.

We used it to wash clothes, the old people's clothes and the bosses'. We never had washing powder like today. When we were washing, we had a washing board — the glass one — we scrubbed it on that. Then they used to boil the clothes in the copper. When you put them in the rinse, you put the blue in the white rag, leave it in there, let him stop and make the water blue. It's good, rinsed out all the smell of that soap. Face soap, that you wash yourself with, he used to order that one. We used to get the round one, nice smell, but you can't get that one any more.

We had irons you put on top of the stove — you might have three. You used one, and put him back to get hot, and you used another one. We only had that one, nobody had electric one. We used to iron the clothes for the two bosses there, Len Smith and Walter Smith, and my father Alex Stewart.

Walter Smith taught us to sew and cut dresses. Say you wanted to make a dress, he used to show us how to fold the material, and where we had to cut, and where we had to put the waist and things, and the hem on the bottom, and the collar. He's the one that taught us. He had no wife. For the bosses, we used to just sew all the buttons and things. In those days, we never had elastic, they only had buttons. We used to sew the buttons, and even a broken shirt that might have got ripped when they were galloping and chasing, we used to sew that. He used to teach us to sew them, patch it up. Any old clothes, get a patch and patch it up. Whatever thing, it had to last for a long, long time, because there was no shop there. Every bit of thing we had to look after them. Not like this time, wasting everything, just going in the dump.

And we used to sew for the old grannies. We used to look after them grannies. Every time when they need something, we might get a material and make a dress for them, or skirt, whatever is. Sometime we make a blouse, but most of the time they like that shirt belong to the men.

Whatever men and women and girls and boys that were working, we cooked food for them all in the homestead. Bread and things, we used to bake it in the homestead. We cooked one lot of meal for everyone, white and black, and he used to carve it all. Put them all in the plate, even the meat and everything, cabbage or carrots, whatever we got. We used to have a dish to take it home, never sit down there. We used to put it all on the dish and go and give it to the men waiting, might be in the big boughshed there. The men were only there for might be twenty minutes and they're off again, see.

But in the homestead, we might be the waitress, we got to work with the two whitefellas. Get everything, set the table and things, get all the food ready for them before we go out. All the rest of the women go out with the food, but we got to wait till we set the table, and when they're sitting down eating, then we get our meal, take them down. We might go home and come back; we clean up the table, wash the dishes and everything. By eight o'clock we finished for the night.

And all the granny and grandfathers, they get a ration, and we used to make a camp fire and cook for them. Walter Smith used to look after all the old people. He used to give all the old people rations free, from the homestead store every Sunday. A little bit of flour, sugar, tea; just from Sunday to next Sunday. Jam, treacle, honey, for the old people. He treated them like that. That's why all the people from the other places come there — they know they get everything free.

They wait till we fellas come, the old people. Sometime if we got any left over from the men's, we used to give it to them. We don't have to cook it then. We used to have big billy like a bucket, boiling: cup of tea all the time. And damper, sometimes we baked it in the camp oven, and sometimes we buried it in the hot sand. Fireplace just in the ground there. Make a fire just in the ground, but you've got to get a special wood so you haven't got ashes, so that meat can be cooked nice and brown. We used to get snakewood — that's really good to cook everything. Nice taste, too. Every morning clean the fireplace. When we finish cooking we bury it in the sand. In the morning we clean it and put a new lot of wood in, and then start cooking again. For sleeping, we had separate fires, near the camp where you go to sleep. We didn't sleep by the cooking fire. You had to make a little fire each side, for sleeping.

Bussoo Bin Abdullah was a British Malay, born in Singapore in 1866, who came to Australia and was registered as a cook at Cossack in 1916, moving to Onslow in 1921. (Australian Archives.)

We had an old Chinaman on the station; he was the cook there 1940s. Bussoo Bin Abdullah, that's his name. He just come look for job there. He talk English good; he used to be nice old fella. He stayed couple of years, but he was getting sick in the tummy, so he went to Onslow Hospital and never come back again. We had a cook room; any cook come, he got a room by himself on the back of the butcher shop. He used to look after the garden too. We used to go and sit in the room, talking to him. He used to be happy to look after the kids. He used to be really nice old man.

We only used to cook an ordinary stew, you know; with the potato and onion and cabbage and things. But when he come, he used to teach us to put the chilli too. We used to have chilli in the garden, and he used to make a curry stew. He used to make us big pot of stew, and used to boil his rice one side. And then he used to cut up the chilli really fine, he just mix it for himself. If anybody wanted, you could use it — he just leave it one side, chilli, cut up one, and the rice and the stew, and he used to give us to taste it. Really nice! Mmm, I like that curry and rice. He used to make it nice, that old fella.

Native Welfare coming round, getting all the half-caste kids

The Smiths were very good people. Soon as someone tell them that Welfare coming, he used to tell us to go down the river now, stay in the bush when the Native Welfare coming round, because they going getting all the children,

For many years of the twentieth century, government policy at both federal and state levels was to remove children of mixed race from their Aboriginal families and make them wards of the State. They were sometimes placed in church missions, often in orphanages, and some were adopted into white families. The policy was to withhold from them knowledge of their true background or family; many were told the lie that they were orphans or unwanted. In principle, these children were to be educated and prepared for participation in white society. In fact, the majority received only a rudimentary schooling and were trained only for menial work; many were shockingly maltreated. In 1997 the report of the national inquiry into this family separation, 'Bringing Them Home', was tabled in both houses of the Australian parliament. The responses to this report are still causing deep shudders in Australian society.

the half-caste kids, take them to Perth. He used to tell us to go bush for a day. We used to be lucky we had a good boss — he don't want we fellas taken away from the mum, from the country. We used to be hiding in the river. He used to go, 'Come on, take it bush.' 'That flash car still there?' 'No, that's gone.' Hamersley and Mulga Downs, all the kids gone. That was about 1930s, that's when it started. And policeman started that time, too, killing all the dogs.

They used to come, I think, because the white-fellas and Aborigine people used to be fighting, and they might have think, 'Oh well, we got to visit all the station, might be some station in trouble.' Might be they was worrying about that, still fighting with Aborigine people. But that's not ... they was good. Station boss used to give guns to the Aborigine people to go shooting, never make him pay. Just give the gun to some fellas. We used to have a lot of guns.

When the policeman come, he take all the guns and shoot all the dogs; we have nothing. That's how bad the policeman is, early day. They just like a mob of army — jump off from the motor car, run straight to the camp. Those days we couldn't understand where they come from. All these policemen come along, they just pick up a trail in the car and they just run straight to the Aborigine camp in Rocklea Station. They shot all the dogs belong to the Aborigine people — kangaroo dogs — and all the mother and the kids crying, going bush, trying to hide away. They just chase them, kill all the dogs: bang, bang, and coming behind you just like a mob of army coming. One time, all the mums and the aunties and people, they just run straight to that place they not supposed to go. Not me, I wasn't there; all the other lot went there. Amy was a little girl then, and her mother was there. That was about 1938, I think.

It was the Law ground near Two Mile, and they went straight there, and they all was in trouble. Women and children weren't allowed to go there. They didn't have a choice then, because this bang! bang! coming behind, knocking all the dogs out, and they think they're getting shot too. They got to hide away in the river. They was running in the flat, in the bush, and they took off to the hill, then they find the policemen still coming, and they

Janjilanha. Sandy Creek well, a popular picnic spot.
Jack Smith's grandfather is buried near here.

went wrong place then. Too late, they all got in trouble. All the people got in trouble; all the husbands belong to them old people.

All the big men, all the head men, when they hear that they cry. They cry that place not supposed to be running with all the womans. It's very strict, those days. Right up to Jigalong they was crying, because this place not only for Rocklea people, this place for all the men that been through the Law, and they all been crying. Women been run into this place. It was really bad.

They never touch anything, they just went right through. But they're still not supposed to go through there. The men went to have a look and they see all the tracks — footprint — went through there, never touch anything, they just went right up to Two Mile windmill;

they had to stay in the water there, away from the policemen. They say that's why there's no one in Rocklea now. All the old people died, all the old people and old ladies, just over that now.

That was really bad. I used to cry and cry, frightened of the policeman. They used to chase the people, but they never kill the people, only the dogs. And we need that kangaroo dog when we got no gun. Soon as they see Aborigine got a gun, they just took the gun off, finished. They used to follow the meeting camps, wherever the meeting camps were; just wanted the blackfella go without gun. And without dog. Well, dog — we need that. We only used spears for hunting then, all the time, the old people.

I couldn't understand what's going on. Those days, even all my mum and my aunty and that, they don't know what's going on. Nobody used to tell us. Even the owners Mr Len Smith, they didn't know what the police were doing, and those days you can't complain. Might be once a year or two days a year, they come around looking whether the Aborigine people making trouble, something like that. Because Aborigines and the whitefellas is fighting before, killing one another, and that's what they was watching, that's what we was thinking. But they shouldn't kill the dogs, that's the only thing we got for hunting food. Dogs are the ones that get the kangaroo and emu, all them things. Lucky the old people used to have a spear; spearing kangaroo, to keep the kids up.

Those days we was very scared about the policeman. We know what sort of policeman been early days, see, when the first Aborigine people and the whitefellas met up about 1870 or 1880, they was fighting. They used to take them away to Rottnest Island, over spearing the whitefellas and things like that. That's what happened before, long time ago, before I born. We still got that in the mind. We know what the families been go through, all the old people, early days. If we do the wrong thing we know the policeman pick us up and take him lockup. We think the policeman pick them up, take them for good, see.

Nobody worried about money much

Nobody got wages. We just work for blanket, sheet, clothes, food, and shirt and trousers for the men. We just work for all that, no money. If we going out from that station Rocklea — say we go to Wyloo Station or Ashburton Station or Mount Vernon — then he used to give bonus money, little bit. Holidays money, enough to buy something in that other place. They used to have a little bit of pocket money, because the boss is very happy how he been working. Done a good job see. Because those old people, when they working they got to put the job really neat, how the boss want them to do it. They used to do it properly. That's the way the old people used to be.

They didn't half finish it and just leave the job and come back next time again, they do that one day, that's finish.

Yeah, that's all he used to give us. Shoe and nail for the horses, everything free. No petrol — all you had was a horse! Nothing to worry about. Got a lot of shoe and nails and hammer and things, that's it. And a bit of grease for the spring-cart or sulky. This was good.

Those days, nobody worried about money much. I never used to worry about money, as long as I eat food, that's the main part, and I've got clothes. We don't worry about going to buy lollies or cool drink — nothing. We never got a cool drink. We only had an orange and an apple when Walter Smith used to get it.

They gave us all whitefella names

Walter Smith and Len Smith just keep using Aborigine names. We got whitefella names later. One of the families from Roebourne, Walter Francis and Mrs Francis, they come to Rocklea, and when they come they call us whitefella name then: Alice, Amy, Dulcie, Mabel, all those. They Aborigine people, but they give us a whitefella name. Mrs Francis, she's the Aborigine, and he's the whitefella, and all the family is Aborigine. They was living in Roebourne all their life, across the river. The two sons was building a shearers' quarter at Rocklea, so all the family come too, mother and the sisters. They used to be helping working, because those days women and men used to work together, so they can finish work. That's only the shearers' quarters they was putting, shearing shed and all them things. They camped next to where they're working.

All our mum and dads got whitefella names, but we never had it. Even Len Smith and Walter Smith, the two bosses in Rocklea Station, they never give us a whitefella name. But now, because there were a lot of whitefellas, Aborigine children got to have a whitefella name so they can call it easy. So Mr and Mrs Francis gave us all whitefella names — that was funny. Then the boss, Walter Smith and Len Smith, they called our whitefella name then. They leave the Bilari one side.

Amy — her name was Moyen*, and Dulcie was Butang. That cook we had, Bussoo Bin Abdullah, he liked all the little girls, and he give Butang her name, and Moyen*. That's in his language. Those two girls never had Aborigine names, and then they got their whitefella name from Mr and Mrs Francis.

They built the shearing shed and the shearers' quarters — I was about ten or eleven years old when they built those. They was shearing with the hand blades. And the shearers used to walk, moving from job to job, wherever the shearing was. They had a spring-cart, but most of the people were walking. You can't all fit in the one spring-cart. All the stuff there. They used to walk; when they get really tired, they get on a little bit, go a little bit, and they'll start walking again. Some shearers used to come on the pushbike, some of the shearers walking. From Roebourne to all around Rocklea — every station — they just walk, carrying the swag. Backpackers! I never used to see the motorbike those days, only bike. Same as the saddling man, fixing all the saddles. He used to do the same, going from station to station, but he used to ride a horse, and he had a packhorse.

They had all the men and the women working like cowboys

A couple of ladies were mustering girls. We used to call them cowgirls; they used to work as stockmen*. My cousin-sister was one of them; they used to be riding horses all the time, helping the men. Whatever ladies that couldn't ride a horse, they do the cooking jobs, and wash up the dishes, and wash all the clothes. But all the ladies that can ride a horse, they got to be out all the time with the men, mustering cattle or horses in the paddock and branding and cutting all the horses and cutting all the cattle. One of them was Delaporte's wife, Inga, and Annie Black, my sister, and one of them my Aunty Dinah. Really like a cowgirl suit, they used to have: the skinny-leg one. And they used to have a belt, and a cowboy hat, and proper high-heeled cowboy boots. Shirt got a pattern different on the chest, and that handkerchief, like a scarf, they used to have it in the neck, hanging down. They used to be really flash, those days. Len Smith and Walter Smith had all the men and the women working like all the cowboys there. Smiths used to buy the clothes, and the workers used to get it for free, because no money those days. Just the clothes and sheets and blankets and pillows and things, for the workers.

Girls were not allowed to break the horses, only men. We used to shoe the horses, all the women, because we might be stuck out somewhere, and we got to be able to do something with the shoe to save the horse to walk again. We used to have a bagful. Nail, rasp, hammer, everything for the horse. And toenail cutter — when they fit the shoe you've got to level that thing, file it with the rasp. We used to do all that.

Fencing: chopping posts, dig a hole, put the post and bore the hole for the fence. That was the girls and the boys. No iron posts, just a wooden-post fence, you've got to chop the mulga trees down all the time. Sometimes we used to make a wire gate. You put two wood in the middle and two wood each side, and you run the wire across — it might be five wires — and that's a gate. We used to make that one. Everybody worked outdoors, boys and the girls. But the young girls were only allowed to go mustering sheep, not cattle and horses, because they're too rough — you've got to chase them a long way.

Mustering plant, Wyloo Station, 1934.
Annie sitting on the wagon, with Dan standing behind.

When they were sheep mustering, we'd all be on the horses then, because sheep are the slow ones.

The old ladies and the mothers used to teach the girls, and the fathers always teach the boys. But the father used to teach the girls to ride the horses too, because they know more than the ladies. He taught us to drive the spring-cart, and how to put the horse in the spring-cart. He used to tell us to stand and watch what he's doing. Don't touch anything, just watch how he's doing it. The father and the mother used to do it, and we picked it up from there. Every morning we used to see them fellas doing it. Next time they used to tell us to do it for ourselves now, 'Try do it yourself,' see how we going to get on. We used to do it easily — all the horses were quiet, they know to reverse back to the spring-cart, the chain and things, and they know to put the reins back to the spring-cart. And when we started driving, they used to just watch.

About 1939, Len Smith got a Ford car. That's the first one we had on the station. We used to like it, too; first time we'd got a motor car. 'Oh, that's a good one,' we reckon. 'That's very good. Better than a horse and cart.' And 1940 he got another little green car. We had two then. No truck, just the two little ones. We were allowed to ride in it; we used to go in the Ford car. We used to have a couple of pushbikes, but not many, you know. When they were broken down we don't know how to fix it! We could fix a puncture, because we got it from the Ford car, we know how to patch that one. But everything else broken down, we got no parts.

We used to have the day off, Christmas

We know Christmas time in the station. They used to tell us, 'This is the Christmas Day today.' They used to get a big case beer — big box, used to be, to give all the people working for him a little bit of drink. Whisky and the wine, them big flat bottle. Only Christmas time, that's all. That's just for the people to have a good party. From that, nothing at all through right up to next Christmas again. No grog used to be in the station, nothing, they used to be clean. That's how we don't know that grog when we was a kid growing up. We seen the beer, but we never used to touch it. We know that thing going to get you drunk. All the mothers used to tell us, and we used to be very scared about that. Because those days kids used to be told not to touch all the bad ones. Even the gun, they used to tell us, 'Don't touch the gun, it's dangerous.' Only the big people can handle them things.

And we used to make a Christmas pudding. We used to have hops, and sometime we used to make our own beer then, for the Christmas. And we used to have a cooler with a bag. We never had a fridge, we only had a cooler, and we used to have everything there. Put all the bottles there, meat and things. We get that pork leg, Christmas time. They used to order it in the mail. Only for the Christmas, that's all. Sometimes when we got a bacon and a pork leg, we boil it in the washing copper for the Christmas. Feed the kids. They used to be good. We used to kill the chooks for Christmas. Only just an apple and banana and lollies for the kids. Sometimes they used to get a big tin lollies, those boiled ones. Whenever Walter Smith used to want to give the kids some lollies, we used to get lollies. Nothing else, no toys. We used to have the day off, Christmas.

We used to have religion own tribal way, no whitefella way. No minister whitefella — nothing. Only Native Welfare and the policeman used to visit us — danger ones! We used to have that *Mingala* thing, we call *Mingala*

Jesus. Tribal way we used to go to them rock carving in the wall. We used to go talk there. We used to tell him to give us everything, whatever we need. And no dangers or anything like that. And we used to be free all the time then. Whenever we do the holiday, that's the time we go to that place. Not often; might be once a year. When working time we don't go there; we work all the time.

4

LEARNING THE TRADITIONAL WAYS

I used to watch the old people and
I learned from there

Holiday time, we used to go out bush, and we used to do our own way, Aborigine way. About four or five mile away from the station, where the holiday camp belong to the old people, we used to go. No windmill around; we were near the Beasley River, where the water is, and sometimes a rockhole. The proper name for that river is Maliwartu. They know, old people; they goes make a camp there. Now, we're living in Roebourne, we're staying here forever. But the old people used to keep moving. Wherever the meeting, they go to the meeting, and all the tribe meet up there, different ones.

We took a spring-cart and a camel; when it's getting late we leave the camel and the spring-cart, we make a fire, get a kangaroo, cook him. Catching the wild food, and doing cooking in that grinding stone. We used to cook a kangaroo in the ashes, and we used to get wild potato and things for damper. We only had a kangaroo dog for hunting, no gun. The wild onion is really good; we used to mash it up raw and put it in the ashes, and he come up like a damper. And we used to get a goanna, cook it. That's all the bush tucker belong to the Aborigine people.

I used to watch the old people doing it and I learned from there. They teach me tribal law belong to whatever tribe, and they tell me all the different tribes and that I'm Banyjima woman, I not allowed to go over to Kurrama or any other language. I got to wait for them to invite me before I can say something about the Law that belongs to them.

No blanket, just dig the sand and make a fire each side and sleeping in the sand, and get up in the morning. Summertime not bad — wintertime you got to have something to cover you up. Before the blanket come, we used to use the paperbark tree from the river. Make a fire each side in the camp where we going to sleep, dig the sand and cover us up with the sand.

If a big general rain coming, two or three days one, we go stay in the cave, because we haven't got a tent and things. We used to move to the big caves in the hill near the river. The old people had special ones they know. Whatever things we had there, we got to take them all up to the cave, stay in the cave for two or three days. Doesn't matter we got clothes and blanket and things, we used to put our blanket and things in the cave. We used to get spinifex and make a bed, so nothing would come up and bite the children. We'd take the food, put them all on the shelf in the wooden dish, keep it dry. When they go out, they cover them with a leaf or paperbark and put rocks round it to hold that thing down, so nothing will get in. We got to stay in that cave, and if we run out of meat or anything, all the men go out hunting through the rain. Just get a kangaroo and whatever they could find. And all the wife and the kids in the cave had a big fire going all the time in the doorway, keep it warm. When they come back to the cave, we'll just cook it just there and eat it. They were still doing it when I was a little girl about ten years old, in the 1930s.

Then, if rain stop, we just got to stay there one more days, let the ground get dry properly, then we move out back to the place where we were before. It got pretty muddy, and nice soft ground now, digging all the potatoes. Get a lot now. Some we put on the shelf in the cave, so no one will get it. We used to make a wooden dish and put them all there. When we hungry we know where to go to get them. Put some stores in the cave, and cover it with that paperbark. It stay there, no one would get it, because it's on a shelf, way up. Even little wild onions, in the dish, the old people used to leave them there. When we're really hungry and we couldn't get anything we can go back and we got the food there, see. But we got plenty sweet stuff. Every day they used to get wild honey. They used to fill the little bowl and keep it all the time. Mix it with the water and have a cool drink or something like that. No fridge, no anything. Only just have spears and boomerangs and whatever little wooden dish they make. That's all they used to keep in there.

No clothes, only kangaroo fur and bird feathers they used to get. They used to get the kangaroo tail, pull the strings all clean, and they used to keep him and let him get dry. They keep strings dry; when they want to use it they put it in the water, soak it, make it soft so they can tie something really tight, and then wax, from the spinifex. Use that one like glue for sticking handle and things — that's to do the spears and everything. Or tomahawk; when they're making it, they use that. It's really good, too.

They used to make wool out of their hair, and they used to make a skirt then. We used to do it too, when we was a little girl. They used to give us a stick and teach us to make the wool. Make a big roll first, like that wool that whitefella doing it, but we do it different way. We use our toe to wind it together, make it long. If it's a skirt, we must make it little bit top of the knees, and then cut it after and make a belt. Skirt will be nice. That's the skirt they used to make, and boys only have got a cock-rag thing, just in the front and the back, nothing in the leg side, and the belt. Before all the whitefellas come up, that's the way they used to be. When the whitefellas come up they had jeans and things, then, but usually they used to do bush way, living in the bush all the time. No shirt, just with the skirt. All their skin was just black with the sun burn.

But when I was a girl I never wear that one. I seen them

making it, still making it to show the young generation coming up what they used to do in the early days before the whitefella come. When I was born I had a whitefella father, and I had clothes and everything, blanket and things. But they used to still do it when we go to bush meetings; in the bush, they used to still do it. They wear them in the *mallalu* time — they call it *mallalu* — the young fella going through the Law. They wear them then, wear that proper belt from the hair, not the whitefella belt. They got to use everything bush way when they putting a boy through the Law.

Early days before the whitefella come, they had a different Law. Say I a woman, when I start getting a period I not allowed anywhere that big mob might be camping. They put that woman with the period separate, one side. She got her own camp. Only the old ladies used to look after, take her food or whatever she want, water or something. That's a secret sort of a thing. No man allowed to go there, or little boys or little girls. She by herself till the period's over, then she come back to the people. She got to be separate. If they moving from there, she got to go one side, and this big mob are going in the one road, and she's got to go hiding all the time till in the next camp. Because those days no clothes — only had the kangaroo skin sort of a thing.

And when she getting a period she got to put a black mark on her face with charcoal. Her husband know then she's getting a period, see. The husband don't do anything, and she move out from the camp, separate, for a few days. Every month, they used to do that. It's very hard, those days, but they know how to work it, themselves. The grannies used to tell me.

They used to tell us stories

When we was living in the bush my mother used to tell story. We'd get outside after tea and we got fire outside and watch the stars and moon and things: story time. They show me the full moon got a gum tree inside — you know the black thing like a tree inside that moon? They reckon that's a gum tree, and possum in there. He always climb on the tree: we call that *walkyi*. My mother used to call, 'That's a walkyi there in that moon, in the gum tree.' And they showed that Milky Way; there's a emu there, in the Milky Way. A black thing there laying like a dead emu.

And there's another little smoke there they show me, a little white one, away from the Milky Way. Two stars there, orange ones that's different to them other lot — that's two young boys went up looking for goanna. The goanna went in a hole, and these two young boys, they start putting a fire inside, making a fire in the doorway, and smoke come out the window at the side. Those two boys is catching the goanna there inside. *Paderangu*, that's the two boys.

And they used to tell us one story about Eagle and the Crow. It's a Kurrama, them two, both of them Kurrama,

Crow and Eagle. They were men then. Eagle's wife is a *kargardi*, a hawk. Eagle and the black Crow went out hunting with all the wife and the kids at home. They went out hunting, chasing all the wallaby, put them all inside the cave. And there was one wallaby that Crow reckoned was his; he was a fat one, he could see the tail all fat. Anyway, they come to the door, and Eagle went inside to kill all them wallaby inside, and Crow staying outside in the doorway. Eagle killing all the wallaby, bringing them all outside, and that Crow reckoned, 'That's not the one mine: mine is the fat one there somewhere. It was a short tail.' And Eagle says, 'Nothing here. *Kanayi*. *Kanayi*, finish,' he reckon. 'Nothing here.'

'Oh.' But he kill that fat one, he put it in the shelf, that's for himself — he getting cunning. And all right, this Crow starts getting wild now, getting hot, too — he know something going on inside. Crow starts getting all the big log now, he getting all the big log, put it in the doorway, block him up inside. And Eagle still looking for wallabies: when he come out to the doorway, he find out he locked up inside, he couldn't get out.

Crow went back home now, pinch Eagle's wife — he took off with the wife! He took off a long way now, taking the wife; Eagle in the lockup, inside the cave. And lucky he had one brother at home — one night over now, and they reckon, 'Where's my brother?' He come looking for him, he could see all the track went there, and he find out he's in the cave inside. He's singing out inside, 'No water.' He was thinking about dying inside. Anyway his brother come up, took all the logs out of the doorway, and dragged him out. He was weak, been eating nothing, no water. He give him drink of water first, his brother, and tell him to lay down. Never give too much, you know, because other way he die, if he have too much drink. And he went out and get the kangaroo, wallaby, now, come back, cook it and give it to him. He had that to eat, and he had a drink of water, and he was still laying down. He went to get another kangaroo now, and he come back and feed him again. All right, they went back home now, after he can walk.

When they walk back home, find out no wife. Wife gone! And all the other lot of wife tell him his wife gone with the Crow. They went *long* way. All right, he been camped there one night in the home, and they going looking for these two now. They climb up in the big mountain, they were singing a corroboree song, but women not allowed to sing that song. They were singing corroboree, to make Crow to start a fire. All right, he start the fire: they can see the spinifex burning, long, long way. They get down from that hill, they walking, keep walking, they climb up on another hill. They sing another song there, different song, they making it, and they sing another song, singing, singing. All right, and they finish, they singing the *karla*, now, that's the fire. Warlumallu, it's a place up north, that's the name in that corroboree what he's singing. Anyway, they seen the fire coming close now, and they come right up where the river is. In the morning before six o'clock they get up, have a look, they see the little smoke coming up from the river now. They was camping next to the river; they had the fire going.

And so these fellas come along then, two brothers. They had a big fight. Fire been burning, everywhere black, and they had a big fight now. The man with the wife, Eagle, he was fighting that Crow. They was rolling one another in that burnt ground, and this Eagle say, 'You going to be a scavenger now, when you got a feather. You going to be the scavenger now. Every kangaroo you see somebody kill him, you're just there for just pinch it.' And Crow started now, do him in the ground — they're wrestling in the black ground. And he said, 'You're going to be a scavenger too, like me, and you'll be eating raw meat all the time.' And they both turned into black and they fly, both of them then, they finish. No more men there. That's the way they come to be black: they was fighting there now. And his wife went flying too, they all finish there. Eaglehawk got black, and Crow got black, and only had the eye white. 'That's all you going to be,' that Eagle reckon, 'and nowhere else. You going to be really black.' He did — he's the really black one now. Crow tell him, 'You're going to be sitting in a tree, or sitting in a mountain, you watch people killing a kangaroo. Everywhere you go, you stop with the man or the woman going hunting. You're a proper scavenger.' That's Crow telling him. He is a scavenger now — you can see him. Wherever the kangaroo dead, you got to see the Eagle or

Crow. They're like that, they was fighting in the bush.

Another story my mother been telling me about the Black Swan and little Chicken-hawk. This Black Swan had the fire all the time, we had no fire then. They reckon that this country was always underwater, when they was around. Anyway, this Black Swan was carrying a firestick under his arm all the time: he wouldn't give other one the fire. *Karlajidu* is the swan, we call him that. Karla is the fire, see. All the other lot eating raw meat all the time, outside of the water — they're trying to get that man to give them fire. He don't want to give it to them, he's swimming in the water all the time — no one can catch him, see.

The next thing all the birds flying, trying to hit that thing from under his arm; diving, trying to take it off him. He's just ducking all the time. But this little Chicken-hawk — we call him *minbirridi*, that hawk, or *miggin*'s the easy one, That's the Kurrama name, *miggin* — he went *right* up, long way away, no one could see him. When he come down, he hit that thing from his underarm, spread it now where all that spinifex is. And there starts the bushfire then. When he start the bushfire, well, country was burning everywhere then; they had fire then, after that. And he had no fire, he was floating in the sea all the time. And this other lot was happy when they got that fire going, and that's the way that man, when he come out, the Black Swan, they got him in the burnt ground, roll him up there, and he's black now — only got a red thing on his face. That's all the story.

Old people used to walk, to put that boy through the Law

There used to be a place called Bourminji-nha, and all the old people used to be there at holiday time; my father and mother used to come visiting them, put the boys through the Law. Holidays they used to have all the old people walking to this place from Rocklea. They all go there, and they used to leave us where the camp is, and they used to go on by themself, have a meeting in this place. Whitefella name was Police Station; it was near Tambrey Station. The policemen used to be looking after the old people there, bring them rations. I never came there, I never seen that place, because I was too little to come there. They used to come to put the meeting through — they used to have the good *purndut*, proper one, the boys' ceremony. They used to help one another. Old people used to walk for that boy, to put him through the Law — they used to be really good, those days. If they don't want to have a purndut, well they used to have all the dance and things.

Before the ceremony, the boy's got to be a long way from the people, he not allowed to see the people in home, and home people not allowed to see him. He got to be taken away till he goes through that Law. Big brother got to be the boss, out in the bush all the time.

That was only in the Christmas holiday, putting the boys through the Law. They do the bush dance, then — all the men — and the women got to be busy in the camp all the time, painting all the mother and father and the uncle and the aunties. Women not allowed to know anything from that bush dance. And all the mothers and uncle and aunty not allowed to walk around when the boy going through the Law: they got to be laying back in bed all the time. They got to be painted every day, they got to sit one place. All the sisters and brothers, they got to cook food for them, they got to make a bed for them. If the women want to go toilet, the sister got to take them. If he's a man, well, man got to take him toilet and bring him back. They not allowed to walk themselves, all the mothers and uncles and aunty. And if they want to go swim — you know, have a bath — someone's got to take them, they not allowed to go by themself. All the women got to take the womans in a different pool. They used to be doing it like that, and bring them back, put a new paint on, this white and red paint. They had a headband and armband, all the colour red paint, everywhere. And hair red. And they got to lay down all the time until the boy goes through the initiation, and then the mothers allowed to go walk around.

After the boy went through the Law, they've got to sing the special song. That's a *wardiba**, they sing that. They started might be eight o'clock in the night, got to sit down all night, right up to six o'clock in the morning, and then they walk the boy to the big mob of mothers then. Sisters and all, meet them then. They sit up all night singing and in the morning they bring the boy to the smoke then.

They have a smoke there, where the mothers is. All the sisters going to grab the boy and put him in the smoke. And from there, that boy, he don't come back and stay with the family, he have to go out with the men then, till they get over everything what they went through. They take him long way, wherever they want to go walk around, till he get better. When he properly good, well he can come back, just walk in then.

And when he come back, that young fella got to go hunting, and he got to see all them dances again, when he bring all the kangaroo in. Only the old people got to go bush and give him all the good dance, show him that dance. That's the end, and he allowed to get married then. That's the proper way. When they go through the Law they got to go away for two or three months till they get over properly. When they come back, they can stay with the women and the kids then. It was good Law, that time.

But he can't just get his girlfriend whenever he wants, because he not allowed to. He got to get permission from his oldest brother. That's the olden day — the old people got to tell him. The old grandmothers can tell the girls too. They got to tell the young girls, 'Don't go for that boy, that boy got to finish all his proper Law first, before you can want him to be a boyfriend. You not allowed to be a girlfriend belong to him till everything over.'

Where I come from, they used to keep it very strict for the young people. Young man's been through the Law, and young girl's not allowed to go and trying to be a girlfriend with that boy. And boy not allowed to see the girls, they got to keep them away. All his brothers always take him away, and after, he allowed to do everything. He got to finish it.

Might be some of them boys don't want to go through the Law. They used to run away, they scared. They never used to catch them — leave it for next time. When he come back next time he might be think everything over, finished. They catch him then, without he know anything about it! That's what they used to do. He got to be fourteen or fifteen, some seventeen or eighteen.

Those days was very strict

The men used to tell us that Rocklea Station had two lots of Law ground. We can't go to that White Quartz Spring — they was hiding things for the Law in the White Quartz. And the other one is up at Two Mile, in the cave; they used to hide it there. And they used to tell us, 'Don't go this way; all the womans and kids and all; don't go to those places.' And all the kids used to know; they used to teach us, because it's dangerous when you go there. They had secret bush gear, and that boy's got to learn about all them things when he's going through the Law, and all the grown up men. Kids always keep away, because those days was very strict peoples. When you do the wrong thing then it goes through lots of meetings and meetings.

Only secret site for women was when they used to have a period and things, and the babies, that's all. Not any secret like the men. That's all they used to have them secret, just the period. That was way back, you know, before I born. That was long time ago, because they had no clothes.

I not allowed to get married to first cousin or anything like that, or my mother's cousin's sister's son. I not allowed to marry them, I got to marry the man away from the family. We got four different colour, see: we got *banaga* — that's me, I'm *banaga* colour. My husband, he's a *garimarra*. *Burungu* got to get married to *milangga* woman and *banaga* got to get married to *garimarra* man, or *garimarra* woman, whatever is. That's the proper way, we can't get married wrong. We got a different Law, you know, in Aborigine way. If we go wrong, well we've got to be in the meeting, and they give us a hiding. You not allowed to do the wrong thing. We got to listen to the old people, what they telling us. Even my family, when they grow up. They still the same; they know. I been teach them: doesn't matter it's not his family, if she's a garimarra woman, she's just like a mother-in-law belong to them, and they not allowed to talk to them, garimarra woman. And garimarra woman's son, he not allowed to talk to me, because he's a milangga. I'm like a mother-in-law. They're allowed to talk to my daughter.

If he's a good man, look after the wife properly, well he allowed to have three wife. If one wife want to leave him, well she can go. If she want to stay, man looking after her, then she can stay. Three or two wife all the time. Well he must have been looking after the first wife, when he got one wife. In a family, you go by the father or grandfather. If this grandfather was cruel to the wife, you know that's part of the family — you not allowed to marry that. Got to be careful. He can be bad all the way, following family, you know. If my grandfather is a bad one, well I going to be a bad one — in the blood, you see. That's they way they used to work it out. They know that that's a bad man.

But those days it was easy, see, the bush tucker all the time. You nothing to worry about, you don't go buying things from the shop. You got three wives, these wife all go different, different ways, get different, different food, to bring all the food to the camp. And husband going hunting. It's nothing to worry about. You don't spend money, you just go and pick from the tree, or might be in the ground, you digging, or goanna, whatever you kill. Because women used to kill goanna and echidna, that's a important thing. Sometimes if pink cocky and white cocky used to have baby, they used to go and get them baby and eat the babies — when they big, you know. They don't get the really little ones. All the birds, whatever birds they could find, cook them in the coal. Get them kids feed all the time. We never used to be hungry, we used to have plenty food, wild food. Potatoes, onions, and the one like the parsnip, we used to dig it in the ground.

Husband and wife, they can go away from the peoples.

They can go camp out one side by themselves, see. They make a camp one side, make a big leaf sort of a thing, make a camping there, away from the people. They used to do that.

If somebody passed away in the camp they always sent the messenger. They used to have one man, he's the messenger. The messenger might go to Mulga Down or Turee Creek or Mount Vernon, or Hamersley. He'll go there one day, get to that place. He travel all day and night, and bring all the people. That day when they bury him, everybody got to be there, doesn't matter if he's not a family. All got to be there for the burial. Where that body been died, they just roll him up and leave him there. In the morning they start to bury it in the cemetery. If it's soft ground, they dig the soft ground near the river or wherever they are. And they put the body in the ground.

They bury it properly, then after they got to clean whatever rocks on the top; they clean it all up. That's the women got to do that — woman job. After, they got to go and get buckets of water, might be four bucket. They sprinkle the water on the top, make it hard like cement. In the morning they go again, every morning they do it, not only the first day. Every morning they got to take that water. If they see the cemetery cracking up on the top, or sink down, they got to fix it up again, make it really good. Put water, harden him up like cement, till two week or three week. When that thing hard, you can't see any crack on the cemetery, well they know that's okay. They put a

Burial cave near Tom Price.

boughshed shade now. Whitefella put him headstone, but Aborigine people put a shelter over the top. They got to watch that — no one got to knock it down or anything like that. They keep watch it.

If it's not soft ground, because they only had a digging stick those days, no crowbar, they used to find a cave in the hills. Might be that man or woman died in the big top of the hill, a little cave there. They used to dig that little cave properly. They used to roll that body in that paperbark tree, and they put it right up to the bottom, flat in the cave they put it. And get all the rocks, big ones, put it all in the doorways, block it up so no dingo will touch that body in the cave. Not many body in the ground; most of the time they used to do it in the hill, you know. Because those days they had no crowbar, they only had that stick. The stick can't dig the ground if it's really hard.

They go there cry every morning. If it's visiting a cemetery they talk their language to this body in the cemetery. They always talk to her or him, all the time, every time they're visiting: 'That's me coming, that's your family coming to do your cemetery.' You got to talk all the time. But kids not allowed to be in the cemetery. Kids could come halfway, but not right up — only big people. They put water in the cup, where the head side, you know, and some bit of food in the little tin. In the morning they come, see nothing there then. When I used to watch them, when I was a little girl, when they first buried that body, they got to leave that food in the head side, and water. Early in the morning they go back, it's all gone. I think that man's spirit gone, too — that main one spirit — he's gone.

They got respect for them cemetery, old people used to be; not like this time. These Aborigine people now haven't got any respect for the people in them. They go bury it and that's it, and dust will be flying on the cemetery, no one go and do something. Later, they go and visit. They check it all the time, through the years. They look after the cemetery properly. If it's sinking down again — you know, body might be getting right away now — well, that thing got to go down. Well they go watch that one, they do it up again, make sure it got to be really good. But they never used to put the flower and things, you know, pretty flower. That's all they used to do: big work, and look after that cemetery properly. Doesn't matter how many years they go away from that cemetery, but when they come back first thing they got to go and visit that cemetery.

All the people that come for the funeral, they come might be one week or two week. All depend they talk about a lot of things after that. If important person been died, they'll have to talk about what's got to come, what's got to do, all them things. If he's important man been died, well they've got to talk about what they've got to do, all them mens, who got to takes over whatever he was doing. And all them other lot when they go back, they know who to contact with if they got any problem or whatever is.

And after, we can't speak that name, more than a year, because the family will be still crying, you know, sad. Soon as they hear the name they cry. Today's different, they can call the name any time, whenever they want. Because we got whitefellas, too — we got to use that name all the time when we're talking to the white people — we've got to call the name. That's the way we come to be changed now.

Everybody used to come to watch the dance

Whoever makes a corroboree song, he's in the spirit. He's reading all that in a dream, getting it through the devil or whatever's giving him the song. And he sees that song like a dream. He see that people dancing in the dream, and singing all the songs. When he get up in the morning, he sing that song, he picturing all that just like he got that thing in the eye, how this corroboree dance goes. That's in the dream, they see it.

That singer is a man: he shows all the dance. They go bush and he shows all this corroboree dance — he might sing this one, well he dance this way. All the dancers know then. He got to be the boss for the team of dancers. Four different skin colours we got. Well, two men, a brother-in-law and a brother, have to be the boss for one team, and another brother-in-law and brother is the boss for the other team. So one team has banaga and garimarra bosses, and the other one has burungu and milangga bosses. That's how we got to go. If they got a new corroboree dance there, everybody used to come from different tribes, to just watch the dance. That was a happy time.

Janjins, yes they used to make those long janjin and the little ones: the little janjins, they go in their hair. And the eagle bird, they used to kill that. They get that feather, they call that *jalyur*, and they put it in the armband. They had a headband made out of a sort of wool made from hair; they used to have that one in the head, and they used to dance with that. And they got a belt, they got to have that emu feather behind. They used to put the tail feathers in the wax, all a heap and all the outside is all spread, like a horse tail. When they're dancing, that thing's shaking behind. That's the emu. The woman make that for the men. Man used to get them and give it to the woman to do it. And you know that white cockatoo? They get the feather from inside, soft ones, inside — clean one. They put it all in the head, then, white one. They used to use some sort of, like a honey, add water, and they mix it and they stick the feathers on their head and body. Then they put paint. All the men paint themselves — the other man paint you, and you paint him, two and two.

We had four paint colours: black one, *kubarru**, yellow one we call that *bijulu*, *mardarr* we call the red paint, and white one we used to call *kakin*. Those four. It was just for decoration, that's all. It's no dangers or anything.

Women used to have the dance too. I used to dance too, when I was a little girl, about twelve, thirteen years old. One of the old lady used to teach we fellas how to dance in that corroboree. We used to paint up everything; we used to have everything, dancing. When the women's dance come, men stay away, only women dance. When the women finish, well, men and women together again, dancing. Like that. You see men dance — just the men — well, women watch the men dancing. No didgeridoo, we only had that

Peter Stevens making a janjin.

Above: Janjins.
Below: Tapping sticks provide the rhythm for songs and dances.
All made by Peter Stevens.

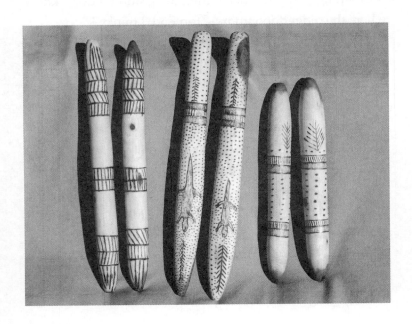

Boomerangs, used for singing and for fighting. Made by Peter Stevens.

boomerangs, and the stick hitting the ground. I don't know where the didgeridoo from — Top End, I think.

They used to clean the dancing ground. No rocks got to be there, for the feet; he might poke with the stone, blister on the foot. They used to clean that properly. Singer — that man used to do all that, and he used to have a couple of people working with him to clean it properly. They used to have a brush shelter so the men hide away behind that, and the women hide away behind the brush. They might be have three for the men, only have one for the women. And they had fireplaces: one in the middle, and another two or three near the singer, and they used to dance round the fire. They used to come out from behind the brush. Yeah — good night, used to be, when we used to dance. Big fire going always.

5

GROWING UP

The old grannies, they're the one who's got to tell us

When the kids were about ten or eleven years old, they know about growing up. Because the old people always used to talk about things in the outside camp fire — tell them how we have to do things, how you've got to go with a *nyuba* — that's a boyfriend. You find a nyuba, and you go with a nyuba, that's your nyuba forever; you're going to have a family, you two fellas. And don't go with the wrong one: uncle or brother or anything like that. You're not allowed to. You've got to go only with the straight man. That's why those different tribes from Rocklea married Yinhawangka people and Nyiyaparli and Kurrama people — mixed marriages. They had to give the daughters and the sons away to the other tribes. Too close was no good, because that's wrong for the old people.

They used to look after every bit of thing, the old people. No one was allowed to do the wrong thing, specially the teenagers coming up. They used to watch them properly. And they used to let us know what my skin colour was, and who were my fathers — *yumini*, in the tribal way — and uncles — we call that *mimi*. We not allowed to go and be girlfriend to that man. These days, I don't know what they're doing; the old ways are finished in Roebourne.

The mother was not allowed to say all those things — only the old grannies. Doesn't matter whether it's not my own grandmother, long as it's a grandmother, and they're the one who's got to tell us. Rough way, too, not a good way, they tell you! Wow, I tell you! This is what she tells: 'You go with a boy, you watch out,' she says. 'You'll be bleeding here,' they reckon, 'and that's no good for you. You want to keep away from the boys till you gets thirteen or fourteen.' They used to tell, 'When you got that period you not allowed to go with a boy, you got to stay away from the boy one side.' They had nothing, early days, but when I was a kid, we could make pads and things from rags, and from that sheep wool too, they used to make it. You know, get all the little pieces been drop from shearing. We used to wash that, and you can put it in the pad. That's what we used to do. Grannies used to tell me when I got a period I not allowed to go with the boys till everything clean. We not allowed to sleep with the husband, too. When we got a period, husband got to have his own bed, I got to have my own bed, till everything stop.

We didn't know birthdays. They used to have a record

when we born, the whitefellas. Aboriginal people go by how big you are, how your body growing. They know I just growing up now.

We used to be frightened of the aeroplane

In the war, all the army planes used to fly through there. And so we see all the planes driving over, and we used to go and hide around the river. We had a wireless thing, some sort, and Walter Smith used to listen that one; where the war, what going on. And we used to have a pedal set, that two-way radio, getting contact with the people wherever the army's fighting. Walter Smith tell us all about what's going on. That's all we heard. Oh, we used to be frightened of the aeroplane — we know that's dangerous, because Walter Smith tell us it's the army plane going up. We was crying when we seen the plane.

We used to get food from Perth in the ship, because no highway used to be, those days. And when that ship couldn't make it — too many army around — we had no flour, no tea, sugar. We only had sheep and bullock there, and we had wild potatoes, but the food belong to the white people, they run out. We don't care; we know what we got. Sometimes we might be lucky to get one of the ships coming from Perth to Onslow. That's where we used to get the food, Onslow. The *Koolinda* is the fastest

Mail plane, Onslow airport.

boat we had. But we used to grind the wheat in the machine like a mincing machine, and make flour out of it. Mix it in the flour, and we used to last that for long time. We used to have brown bread all the time! Flour is finished, sugar is finished; we used to get wild honey. Take a while after the war before it's normal. Still scared about the submarine or whatever is in the water.

When they bombed Darwin, my cousin was there, Leary's oldest brother. He went from Rocklea Station — he had that leprosy — to Derby. From Derby he had to go back to Darwin to take the ship back to Hedland. But the day that he was catching that ship to come back to Hedland, the Japanese bombed that place. He got bombed there. And died.

When the war finished, we had a mail plane running

then. First we'd only seen army planes, and we know that's dangerous. We go hide around the bush. And then Walter Smith say this war's over now, it's finished. We're going to get the mail plane. And we was all right then, we know that's the mail plane coming.

He teach me how to look after the husband

Those days they never used to let the young people to get married early, you know. I got to live with an old man first, and he got to teach me how to look after the husband. Bob — Widdaberi — that's his name, he's the one taught me. The same old fella been look after my sister first, Annie Black. She was staying with him. All right, then she went and find Len Smith, that's her boyfriend; they got a son. When she was living with him, the Aborigine man took off then. She was pregnant then for Len Smith. And this old fella said, 'Well, you can go, my nephew can look after you.'

Then I was living with him for a while, and he teach me how to look after the husband, how to work with the husband. For a couple of years, and then I went with Jack Smith, and he had an old lady teaching him how to look after the wife. I allowed to have a boyfriend, but you're not allowed to go and live with that young man till you get the okay from the older people. Then you can go and

Inga and Mabel Tommy (Paterson).

marry that man. You got to wait for the okay first. That old fella, when I left him to go with the proper man that I can have family with, he just say, 'That's all right.' He don't follow me. He might get his own wife, same age as him now. Proper wife, or another young girl, or somebody.

Jack Smith lost his mother when he was twelve years old; his mum died. He used to be a packhorse man, when he was eighteen, and he used to look after himself. He used to be dogging, killing all the dingoes, and he was an independent man all the time. He was in Rocklea when I was growing up.

He had a old lady first, Inga, and then I come along. She never had children with him, she had children of her own, old ones, with another husband, a whitefella. That overseer who used to be in Rocklea: Delaporte. That's the father of her son. She was an Yinhawanga woman. She like a teacher, you know. Middle-aged woman understand about everything, give him all the idea how to go with the wife. They was running round when Jack Smith was young — I think he was only eighteen or nineteen when he was running round with that old lady. The old people tell that old lady she can look after him, teach him all them things.

Then he start work with one of the whitefellas; he used to do all the fencing and things. He went up to Kooline Station, did the fencing there, and he come back to Brockman again, have a look around his country we been living in. Bulygudi, we call that country, and Nharraminju, on the other side of Brockman Station. That's all his land, Kurrama land.

My husband born top of Brockman hill

When Jack's mother grown up, mounted police used to go with the horse riding, chasing all them Aborigine people to want to take them back to the stations. They want the Aborigine people to stay in the stations, but Aborigine people been wandering round before the whitefellas come — that's their area. They go wherever they want to go. They had no home, they just go there and there. That's their country; wherever they belong,

Mount Brockman. There is a spring on the mount called Bulluru.

well they go camp in a different spring, or get up to the mountain to look for something.

Mabel Tommy's husband was born on Mount Tom Price, right up the top, because the policeman chasing them. They can't leave the wives where policeman coming all the time — she might be having a baby, policeman run in. Policeman used to come really bad there. So they go and camp there, and that's why the baby used to be born on top of the hill so policeman can't find them, see. That's the secret place belong to women!

Mabel's husband been born in top of that big range, and my husband been born in Brockman, right up the top. That's how he named *Bulluru* — that's the name of that country. In Onslow, they used to call him Bulluru

Jack Smith; that's his proper name. You can see it in Onslow Police Station — Bulluru Jack Smith. Bulluru his Aborigine name, Jack is the whitefella name, and Smith for his father.

Mabel and Algy Paterson.

6

MARRIAGE AND FAMILY

We was married properly then

So I move to Jack Smith and I was okay then; I allowed to go with a young man. I never been promised, we just a boyfriend and girlfriend first. And then he started working with another station; he wanted to do the cattle mustering and contract and things on Juna Downs Station.

George Park, he was the boss in Juna Downs Station, and he used to do all the contracts for Turee Station and himself, mustering cattle in the Turee River, all around the Turee boundary. He used to brand all the cattle, and so my husband went over there and helped him through that mustering when he was on holidays. And that's where we was married properly then, when I went to Juna Downs. Aborigine way married, not the whitefella way. The old lady was still there, because she was a nanny then, for the family.

George Park was good to work for; he was a whitefella. We was mustering there right through to the next year. It was really nice. We met lot of different people, different tribe language — they was all there. We stayed in the camp near the homestead. Just a spinifex building, all the boughsheds and things, and camp fire. We was cooking the damper and everything in the camp fire, and we used to go round mustering.

*My husband's father, he tell him
to go live in his own way*

Then we come back to Rocklea again, and we went to the outcamp, a long way from Rocklea, at the boundary. Gabbo — it was an outcamp belonging to Rocklea, but we were just killing dingoes now, no more station work, mustering or anything. Len Smith, my husband's father, he tell him to go live in his own way, whatever way he like it. So he was killing dingoes and things in the outcamp near Paraburdoo. Water and everything, windmills everywhere there, and a spring. We had to camp there all the time, stay there all the time in our own ways.

It was really good. You got garden and everything you can make yourself, do what you want to do. Go out hunting bush tucker all the time. We used to get kukutarri* — like a carrot, but he's a white one. Nice, too. And we used to get lots, lots of witchetty grub; lots of goanna we used to kill whenever we want something for a change.

And lots of wild fruit. We used to go hunting something like a parsnip, but a bush one. It's like a potato inside, you cook it. If we wanted a kangaroo, we used to have a kangaroo dog to hunt it.

When we was in the outcamp in Gabbo, we had big garden. Tomatoes, strawberries and gooseberry — sweet one — but we never had a lemon tree or orange tree or anything like that. We had pumpkin, watermelon, cabbage and all them cauliflower and things. Cucumber, and that big pumpkin, butter pumpkin. Really hard one, and sweet! We used to bury them in the sand — they was nice. I love pumpkin.

We was three wives, then

And Amy, then she come after, but that's a given-away wife. Amy, she young; she was thirteen when she come to the husband — she was promised. He had to take her, because that's a promised wife. She was Yinhawangka as well, the same as Inga. We could have walked out, but we didn't want to do that. No good for the old people; hurt their feelings, see. They'd think we're getting cheeky to all the family. A lot of spear was flying for marrying and things, those days. That's in the tribal law. We can't kick her out, whether we like it or not, we got to keep her there. We was three wives, then.

My husband used to go camping all the time, camp out in the bush, long way away, and leave the family in the camp. He was killing all the wild dingoes in the back country. We used to put the bait on that dingo trap in between the two teeth, you know, in the edge, and when the dingo come, he put his foot there. Say this is the dingo's path, jumping over a log; well you've got to put the trap this side, so when he jumps, he's straight into the trap. The trap will always be tied up in the tree, and we'd cover the wires on the ground so he won't see them. When he gets caught, then he can't drag that trap away, he'll be there forever and die. We used to have lot of dingoes. We'd get the dingo ears and tail, give it to the station, and station sent it in the mail to Ashburton Shire in Onslow, and they get the money then. That's all the money we used to get.

We used to be three or four people in that camp. There's Amy, and the old lady, and Jack's brother and his wife — my cousin, Dora Gilba — and any other man — they might come from different places. They want to stay there, we'll keep them there. Some come from Juna Downs, some might come from Turee Station. They used to visit us. They stayed there for little while, then they go back whenever they want to. We'd go back to Rocklea Station to get our food. We fixed all the boundary windmills for them, but we had the bush camp all the time now. We used to have a spring-cart and a horse. All through, we had a spring-cart and a horse; that's all we had right up to 1948 or '49.

There were only bush tracks, station ones. You couldn't drive a motor car much, you know, because of the punctures. And we used to drive the sulky or a buggy, to go out bush. If not, well we used the packhorse, and we used to walk leading the horse, if we had one horse, enough to carry the swag and the food where we wanted to go. We used to lead the horse and walking. Those days the old people used to walk for a long, long way. No knee trouble or asthmatic or anything. They used to walk miles.

Two kids been taken away from Rocklea

While I was in the boundary, out in the outcamp, I heard from the station that two kids been taken away from Rocklea. Good few people was there, but nothing they could do about it, because the Native Welfare and the policemen used to be really bad, those days. Len Smith, he would have known, but there's nothing that he could do to bring them back. It

Nelson Hughes, 1995.

was Peter Stevens' brother and sister, Mick and Ida. George Park was the father. The mother belong to them, she was blind and she was a little bit mental; she don't know what she's doing. We been foster of them kids; we was looking after them.

And what happened, their own grandmother, Maggie Bimba — that's Amy's mum — been report to the Welfare. She was getting jealous over Len Smith, because Len Smith the boyfriend belong to her, and she don't want Ida to go with Len Smith. She was getting jealous and so she asked the Welfare to come and pick them two fella up, take them to Carnarvon mission. And we was very cross, very wild about her, because she didn't look after them two — we been looking after them. She just complain because she don't want to lose Len Smith. They was big: thirteen and twelve, and they never come back. Even at Christmas holidays they never come back. We lost them right out. Welfare don't sent the letter back where they are, what place they're staying, they don't send that for mother or the family. They just keep it secret all the time. And they tell them they don't know who their family, see.

Alice never realised how fortunate she was not to have been taken away, and that the Native Welfare officers were well aware of her existence. In 1940 she was listed by name in a memo, with a recommendation that she and others should be apprehended and taken to Moore River Native Settlement as soon as possible. Later memos described her living in a married state with a middle-aged man, and later again married to Jack Smith, so she was never removed.

My two cousin-brother, Nelson Hughes' brothers, those two been taken away from Hamersley. Bedford and Jackson, that's the name of those two boys. They was twelve and thirteen. And four others been taken away from Mulga Downs Station: Sue Bigley and Ronnie Mills and two cousins belong to them. They're one family; four kids been taken away from there. They changed their names and everything. Sue come back when she had two, three children. She never used to go visit the mother and father or her grandmothers or aunties, because she don't know nothing about the people.

Losing kids, see their kids crying, going in the car. They was crying. They couldn't do nothing. They just put them in the car, take them away. From that day, you never see them again. Till they grow up big, I don't know how many years.

We just have a baby and that's it

My husband went to Mardie Station to help someone there, in 1944. I was pregnant with our first son. And when he there, he seen the big cyclone. That's the first time he seen a cyclone; we don't know the cyclone, we never used to get it in Rocklea. And he made a song about that then. Jack Smith was famous for making songs about anything special that happened. Mardie Station's flat, all covered up with the water, and he sung for Mardie. I was in Wyloo Station waiting for him. Lucky I never come, because I was just one more month waiting for have a baby. Then we went back to Rocklea, and I had the baby there.

I had my first child, Des, in 1944. I was about twenty, I think, or something like that. No sickening those days. No, we used to work. We had a big garden there. And we used to go walkabout. We used to walk for ten mile or twenty mile and come back to home again. Those days we had no stuff or anything to stop from getting a baby. No bush medicine, nothing. No, they got to go till they stop themself. Like me, I had nine children, and they stopped self. Some of them only go maybe five, or two kids.

When I pregnant, some food I not allowed to have, doesn't matter I'm hungry. I can't have that, because of the baby. This is the wild turkey. Not allowed to eat when you got pregnant. And this big plainy kangaroo — big kangaroo — you not allowed to eat that. Only that brown hill kangaroo — euro — you allowed to eat that. And echidna, you not allowed to eat that; goanna, you not allowed to eat that; fish, you not allowed to eat that. That fish got a bone, see. If I swallow a little bit of bone, it goes in my baby's throat — that's what they used to tell us. Turkey, it make the baby skinny, because all his rib part is skinny, that turkey, and baby going to be not healthy when he born. Even that plainy kangaroo, baby going to be humpy back like that. That's what they used to say: baby won't be strong. If you eat that hill kangaroo one, he's good

— that's a strong one. Goanna, he no good for the mother. He give you plenty pain when that day that baby want to come, in the labour. Echidna mean he'll be slow baby walk: won't be crawling, you know. Might be eighteen months before he can crawl, because echidna is a slow one. That's how they used to tell us. It was really hard time, those days, and no food. We had to find something from the tree, or *bardi* — the witchetty grub. That's what we used to eat, for the pregnant people. Some sort of wild onion or wild honey, make a cool drink. Good enough for people, to keep them up. Very hard, those days.

We call that *nganjali*. Nganjali, that means we don't eat that, only eat whatever things we allowed. We allowed to eat emu when we pregnant. When we born the baby we stop eating emu till they paint the baby and the mother with black stripes and footprints all over your body, and you're allowed to eat that then. But he's got to be two or three years old first, that little one. If they get this plainy kangaroo, I not allowed to eat. Doesn't matter if I'm hungry, I got to keep away from that, because that's better for the baby, that's what they used to tell us. We used to take notice of old people, because they're right, they know. They've been going on for years. We been following all the old way when we was in the station. We still got to follow the own way, that tribal way. We can't put that one side.

We allowed to eat sheep, because sheep got nothing to do with the Aborigines. Aborigine people got kangaroo and goanna and echidna and all them things all the time, before the whitefellas come. Not bad when we got the flour and tea and sugar; then we was all right. We stopped eating that special kangaroo, but we still had flour, tea, sugar, damper. That was good then. Pregnant people still got something to eat. Sheep and bullock meat, we used to eat. But the important thing was that bush meat, we not allowed to eat that. When the baby's out, you're all right, you can eat them stuff now. But this time I think is too much tablet and things, needle and things. When they find out something wrong with the mother they give you tablet or must be needles. I think that's the one making it no good for the kids, even the little babies. I don't know, but I never been living in them.

When I have a baby, my husband's not allowed to be there. All the men not allowed to be there, only a couple of ladies — they got to be there with me if I having a baby. We had to have two ladies looking after us. One's the midwife, and the other one might be just getting water or bringing the lunch for that midwife. That was Amy.

Those days we never used to worry about dying or something, or killing a baby or anything. We just have a baby and that's it. No stitches, just straight out, doesn't matter how big. Might be a ten-pound baby, well he's just got to come out the normal way. They don't cut it or anything, those days. If I'm having trouble, if I'm having pains all day, at lunchtime we might order the witchdoctor to come up and do something, and baby comes faster then. That's what we used to do — get a witchdoctor. No medicine, he just puts something to drive the baby down. Puts something on your tummy and pushes down with his hand. And he was good, too, those days. Well, we were all born in the bush, anyhow. All my relations, we've all been born all around Rocklea, everywhere in the bush.

Well, I had the first one near the outcamp, and I only was a skinny woman then. When I felt pains I just told the midwife to take me in the bush, away from the kids and all the men and other lot, stay by ourselves till the baby was out. Out in the bush, in the sand. The old lady, Inga, was the midwife; she looked after three of my kids: Des, Eva, Marshall. She's the one was showing me how we have the baby in the bush, how you've got to cut the cord and things. We have the baby sitting up on our knees, and when the baby's coming, he just comes the normal way out, into the soft sand. They've got to wait till everything comes out first — they don't cut the cord before the bag comes. Everything's out, and the bleeding comes, well that's when we cut that cord, and then we make a big hole and bury it all right there. And the cord, cut it not short, cut it long a little bit.

The old lady taught me to bury the baby bag, and all them things. That's how it used to be; she's the nanny now in the camp. If she goes somewhere else, she takes the kids with her, whatever kids about four or five years old. The kids like to go with her, wherever she wants to go. The kids used to follow her.

And that lady that's looking after me, she's the one who's got to do all the cleaning the baby, putting him in the bed, and baby's not allowed to have milk till might be after lunch or sometime — everything's got to be cleaned. They turn the baby first, tip him and pull everything out from his face, then they put their finger right up to the throat, clean all the rubbish out. But they've got to have a clean finger all the time, to do that.

Right, one more thing they've got to go and look for now: cork tree, *kartan**. They've got to get some bark from that and burn it, make it black. When it's black they rub the baby and make that baby go really black. Like a powder, you know, they put it all over them everywhere, he's got to be black all over. Mix it in water. Don't mix it in oil or anything, just mix it with water, and rub him with the hand. It's no good for the eyes, they reckon, if you put it in oil or something. Only put it in water and cover him up all over. You only could see the eyes shining. Do it every day; after you bath the kid, you do it again, and they reckon that's really good. All my babies never died; none of them died, and I had nine kids. I was doing it like that all the time.

For the little one, too, they put warm sand on the legs and things like that, to make it little bit hard, because he's too soft, that little one. Every morning they've got to make a fire and rub him and hotten him up all the time: legs and face and everywhere. They reckon then they'll get strong, so he could grow up quick. Every morning you see the mother doing it like that. Those days they used to be really careful with their kids. Same as me; when I had all my kids I used to look after them myself. I don't give them to other people to look after.

And the cord, when it comes off from the baby, they've got to keep it rolled up in a hanky or something, and when it's dry, keep it till the baby starts walking. They've got to put it in wax — they melt it and they soak the cord and make it soft again, and flatten that wax, put the cord inside, fold it up and put another one on the top and make a little hole for a string to hang on the baby's neck, and he'll have it like a necklace. Playing with it till he's around two or three, and when he's about three years old I've got to take it back and make a hole next to where I buried that bag. Mash it up there and bury it there. And that's finished, then, all together. That's what we used to do. He's got to be three years old, because at two and one he's got to play with that necklace thing.

We got to follow that tribal way properly. We not allowed to bring the baby home straightaway when we born the baby; we got to keep it out for a while, for a week or two weeks, before we come to the people. And baby got to be really clean and shiny. Then everybody allowed to see. Even the mother got to be clean, then she allowed to come to the people then. We used to be careful.

We gave our kids both names; Aborigine name and whitefella name. Where they're born, under the tree or one of the springs, that's their country, that's their place, and that's where they've got to called. For the whitefella name, we just picked a name we'd heard about. 'Oh, that's the name I'm going to put on my son or daughter.'

Amy was thirteen when she got Gladys, and no hospital. She was only *little* — very skinny little one, and everybody was getting scared, all the old people in the camp. Me and my cousin-sister, me and her was sitting all night, and she having the baby out in the bush. We can't leave till we got the baby out. Baby was big, and we was scared, too, but we had to help somehow. We was helping her all night and right up to eight o'clock in the morning.

Just pushing and pushing, and when I felt sleepy I put my foot behind her back to push it like that! Put it with my foot, and my cousin-sister, she was doing it in front. While we were doing all this, we had to call the uncle's name — he's got to be the brother of that woman having a baby — we call them *karyardu**, sort of a godfather. And so the baby come out very quick then. Sun up, and she was born then, Gladys. Then she was all right.

Yeah, it was a long night, sitting up all night right up to next morning. We couldn't leave her, because no one wanted to help her. We had to put up with it and look after her. Eight o'clock we was finished. Oh, that was a bad one. When we finished that we went to sleep then! One of the old ladies came up and did something about looking after the baby while people were having a sleep, till everybody woke up okay again.

The breastfeeding, it's a problem too, because those days we had no bottle. But we used to get a special stuff to rub everywhere, to get that milk going quickly. You get the little bag of droppings from the nest of the finch bird, put it in water, and it goes like a milk. And you rub that all around her breast, and the milk comes then. Really good. You've got to get that stuff to rub all over the mum to get that breast running quick. Only that finch, not just any bird, only that one. All the little ones in that nest, they drop all them things, and you get that clean top one, and tip this one in a very little water in your hand, and rub it up, and then put it all over the mum. Then you see the milk come fairly strong. Otherwise you will lose the baby, because you can't feed him. Sometimes we used to mix the powdered milk, but that's in the whitefella time. But before, just keep him up with the water, mix a little bit of wild honey in the water, just to keep the baby up till the milk come up. Keep him full, you know.

If somebody there's got a baby, well this new baby can have the milk from that mum for a while, till the new mother have her own. We usually do that. This new baby, he got to pinch the milk from that baby, now! We sharing like that. We feed them till they're four years old, all depending how long you want to be in the milk.

From 1942 we were in the outcamp right up to 1948, then I had Eva. They was all going to the Law meeting in Mulga Downs Station, and I had no one to stay with me in the outcamp, so Jack brought me back to Rocklea Station and left me there. Lot of ladies there, old people. Amy was there; she used to look after me then. I had Eva not far from the homestead, this side of the woodheap, just in the flat. Wintertime, you see. She was born at night-time. Early in the morning they brought me back to the old ladies' home, where they had a boughshed. And the rest of them went up to the meeting in Mulga Downs Station, Law meeting, because one of the boys was going through the Law.

Then they had no job to give us

After that, in 1949, Len Smith died, my husband's father, and Walter Smith his brother, the old fellow, couldn't look after the station by himself. He had to sell that station in '49 or '50 — sell it to the people from Cane River. And they bought that station. When the new boss come, he was a different one, never had Aborigine people working in the station where they come from.

We was getting kangaroo skins now; dingoes and kangaroo skins. And so we was just wandering around killing dingoes and kangaroos. We had no money — we never was in the social service or anything like that. We were still in Rocklea, but there were new people in charge. We came back to the station again, in 1951, to show them all the windmills, because those people didn't know where all the springs and things were. We was working there only just one year, then they had no work to give us in the station. They tell us no more job. Well, we moved to Wyloo Station, then: 1952.

7

WORKING LIFE IN THE BUSH

Everybody just went off

At Rocklea, the new boss didn't want all the Aborigine people to work there, because no more sheep, only just a little bit of cattle and horse. We used to get ration every Sunday from the station, you know, because we had no wages or anything. All the boys used to work, sheep mustering and cattle mustering, they only get little bit of money, bonus for them. But all the wife and the kids, we used to get the clothes and blankets and sheets and everything free, and tucker, all ration.

New manager, he don't want to keep too many people in the station; everybody just went off. Not only Rocklea; the same lot of boss was in Coolawanyah and Mount Florance. People from Mulga Downs, people from Mount Florance and Coolawanyah, they all moved out. All the young people were still looking for work, because they like horse riding all the time. They went to Nanutarra, Bullaloo, Mount Stuart and Ashburton, and later they all

Morning tea at Minderoo Station, 1949.
Left to right: Alice Smith's mother Maggie, Syd Smith, Eva Black,
unknown friend of Syd Smith, Alan Black, Ian Black, Elizabeth Black,
Charlotte Stream, Cathleen Hubert, Annie Black, Scotty Black (standing).

move to Onslow, then, settle down in there, because the old people went first. My mum was there, holding the Reserve for people to come in.

My mum had been at Minderoo Station and stayed there, working. My sister died, and two children about six and five, and my mum looking after them. She was in Minderoo working, just helping gardening and something. Mervyn Forrest, he was the boss in Minderoo

Wyloo Station homestead and stockyards, 1934.

Station. Then Native Welfare asked my mum to put them
two kids in Onslow school, try see how the two Aborigine
kids would go. They was going good, so my mum moved
from Minderoo Station now; the two kids going to school
in Onslow, and so she moved to Onslow Reserve.

That's my mum, the one start that Reserve in Onslow!
She only was living in the tent — the Welfare bring a tent
there for her, and one little tank. Where all that Bindibindi
village now, that's been the Reserve. She only had that
little tank and a water tap, and whatever she had in her
tent, and all the fireplace the same as we used to have in
Rocklea. She had a tent house and the two kids and her
and the husband belong to her. Not a proper husband,

just a boyfriend, them two living together; someone there to look after her. Grand daughter and grandson, they was going to school there. And when they turn thirteen, they move to Carnarvon Mission then, and she was by herself in the Reserve then, with her husband.

Then Aborigine people went there from different different places, mainly from all around Mulga Downs and Rocklea, Kooline, Wyloo; all settle down in Onslow. They only had a one big building — that's the office and things, look after the food — but all the people used to live in the boughshed and the tent houses, that's all they had. Tin shed laundry and everything, bathroom, they had it in one unit, big one for everybody. And they want a shower, they got to go to that place. And then after, they built the little houses then.

My mum was like it, because she'd been that long in Minderoo Station not far from Onslow. In Onslow she used to do a little bit of work, might be washing clothes for somebody, because those days hardly had a washing machine. Hand wash, you know, and hanging the clothes and things. Or clean up the yard or something, gardening. That's all she used to do. And get a little bit of food from them, and little bit of money. That's what she used to do. I don't think she had a pension; those days nobody had a pension or Supporting Mother or Family Allowance.

One week, one mile fence in the hard ground

We went to Wyloo first, then the first fencing contract started. Just keep moving from station to station, just doing the sheep yard, fencing, and cattle yard. Station owners know all the fencing men. They used to ring us up, send the message from there to Rocklea or wherever we are, and then certain day we got to be there. My husband got to go out with the manager first, to have a look where we got to work. All the stations about the same.

One of them storekeepers, friend belong to my husband, sell us the Chev truck, the old one. That's the one we dealing with all the kangaroo skin and dingo and things in Onslow. Whatever we get, gold and things, we sell it to him, and so he tell us, 'You can buy a truck.' And so we got that truck, second-hand one.

Before we can get money, we got to put three mile fence. We used to do one week, one mile fence. We got to work two, three weeks before we get paid. If everything finish, then the boss come see that, measure how many miles that fence, and then you know you've got your money. If you run out of food you can go to the station — sometimes station used to help us; if we run out before the money, they used to give us the food from the station. It was hard, very hard. Lucky we got kangaroo and everything there, you know; all my kids never used to be eat too much food. They used to live on the bush tucker more, looking for food and things, wander round.

One week, one mile fence in the hard ground, if we driving all the wooden post. Lot of work in the fencing. Wooden one, you got to go and chop the tree down first, then chop it all up, and then you put them all in the truck. And someone got to go and put all the marks along the line where you got to put all the posts. And you got to go grabbing all the posts now — one in the back of the truck and the other one driving slowly — drop all the posts in there and there where all the marks. And then after that you got to go and dig the ground to put the posts up. And this is a crowbar job, too. If we got iron posts, that only take us about two, three days, and that's the easy one — you can just drive it all along, just like you're running. All you got to put the wire in, and that's it.

Not bad when we was in Kooline — we had everything machine work. Hole digger, and that's the same machine for boring the hole in the wood to put the wire through. We was lucky there, and it's marsh country there, soft country. But when you're coming into the hilly country, rocky country, that's the bad one. Yeah, you've got to do it with the hand in Mulga Downs. You've got to dig them with the crowbar there, and put the fence up, and you got to bore it with your hand, brace-and-bit. Oh, lot of work, and the country very hard. Take you two or three weeks before you finish everything.

They never been getting sick

But Rocklea old people used to be very strong ones. You know, they used to be hard for work. They work all day. We used to work from six to six, but we have lunch in the line where we're working, not going home. Just have a little bit of lunch and start again. If I have a baby, baby got to be under the tree, newborn baby. It was a hard work.

I never used to stop working. I think because we was living in our own food; never been touching all the orange and apple and bacon and things like this now. We only used to live with a bag of flour, tea and sugar, and jam and the bush tucker most. When I have a baby, might be eight o'clock in the night, eight o'clock in the morning I start working. That's how we used to be, out in the bush life. We was out by a pool of water in the bush, just making a brush boughshed, and keep all the kids there. And playing in the sand all the time, not clean. Whenever they want to play in the sand they allowed to go play in the sand.

This time, if something wrong with the baby, or mum's weak, they got to be in the hospital two or three week. That's new for old people like me. I got nine kids, none of them died. And we been using all the bush medicine all the time, and the witchdoctor. That's all we had. Those days we had no hospital, anyway, only Onslow and Hedland and Roebourne, too far. I have a baby I might be one week just working little bit of jobs, and then I got to start full. My baby used to be under the tree, in the hot middle of the day. Christmas, all through. And they never been getting sick or anything like that. That's how bush life is. And we don't know lollies and all them food what we getting now. All we know: damper, meat, jam, tea, sugar — that's all, nothing else. No cold drink — if we want a cold drink we used to chop the honey down, tree out in the bush, make a cold drink. That's how we was working there. It was good.

And 1952, I had three kids then. I was pregnant with Marshall when we was working Wyloo Station, fencing. We was going to hospital now, because Marshall was overdue. My husband said, 'We might as well take you to the hospital then.' We come back to Hamersley, drop one old fella Hamersley Station. When we going back they start got worried. We make a camp — because no light in the truck — and Marshall start give me the pain and I just go to bush and have it straightaway! Probably bumpy road, because those days no graded road, just the bush road. And Marshall was born in the creek at Mettawandy, on Wyloo Station. He was not a lot trouble — easy. Same midwife I had, that old lady. Jack was there; he helped. Me and Jack and that old lady now. Couple of kids, that's number three, Marshall. One of the ladies, station boss's wife, call him Little Mettawandy — that's his Aborigine name.

We just wander round, chasing jobs. After Wyloo we went to Kooline Station; we been there for long time, putting all the sheep yard and the fencing. We always lived out from station; we don't live in the station when we working. We start the camp here, if we got five mile fence finish, we got to move to there, now, to finish that fence off; another camp. From there, another camp. Keep packing up all the time. We had the old truck, and we had a kerosene freezer now; we had no fridge before. We had beds then; them old cyclone beds. We used to make a shade in the truck, and when we camp, we make a boughshed and put the brush right round. Put the brush leaf outside first, and then put all the spinifex in the middle and put another leaf outside and tie him up with the wire then — hard work.

When we get money we keep it just cash. No bank account or anything; we don't know the bank account! Len Smith and Walter Smith teach us the money count; two bob, ten shillings, two pound. We know that. Whatever money we get, we had a cash-box thing, one with a key. We always lock it up there, we keep it ourselves. Because those days nobody worry about money much, you know. Like me, I never used to worry about money, long as I eat food, that's the main part, and the clothes I got.

My husband used to fix the engine himself, out in the bush: get another engine and put it on, go again. Those days we used to have lot of whitefellas running round in the bush; gold digger and Kooline lead mining people, things like that. If the car broke down we used to go see them to get a part. They used to have a lot of old motor cars, dead ones around, and my husband used to get a

Loading cattle, Onslow jetty.

part from there then. We used to be all right, then, because he can fix the motor car himself. And that how all my boys, when they broke down or engine something wrong, they pull the engine by themselves. No driver's licence those days. You could drive right up to Onslow — no driver licence!

Those days we was very scared about the policeman. If we do the wrong thing we know the policeman pick us up and take us lockup. We think the policeman pick them up, take them for good. That's what happened long time ago, before I born. We still got that in the mind, see. We know what the family been go through, all the old people.

They used to take them away to Rottnest Island. We still got that olden day in the brains, how they used to be rough-handle them. We was scared about the white people, we was scared about the policeman, and the Welfare. We still picturing from what the policeman done when I was ten, eleven years old. I still can see the river, all of the camp we used to have, and policemen just running with the .303 and blowing all the dogs and throwing all the blankets and things, looking for guns. But when I had my family and husband we'd go to Onslow, we used to go in the street, and we was all right then. We was settling down now.

We had the biggest shock when we seen the sea, because in our country we're used to river water. When we see the sea, oh no, we think about the old people been in this boat and they take them to the island. We used to think about all that, and we used to see the ship standing in the jetty, Onslow.

People been tell us. 'That's sea water,' they used to say, 'sea water is not fresh water like we fellas got. They salty one, yucky one. Even part of the sea coming creek, you not allowed to drink them water, till you go way up, long way from that sea water, then you get a good drink of water.' We never used to go fishing; we frightened of the sea water! Only we used to fish in the fresh water. Later we was all right. We see all the other people go fishing; we go fishing then. Stand in the edge of the lagoon.

When we went to town we spent whatever money we

got. We spent all that money there, come back with no money, long as we got food and the petrol and oil for the motor car things. Start all over again. That what we used to do all through the year, running around like that.

He think about whitefellas not classing him out

Then my husband got his Citizenship Rights — that's what they used to call the 'dog licence'. That was about 1955: you get like a driver licence, but he's a big one, you know. There was a picture of his face on that Citizen Right. And when he had that Citizen Right, my husband allowed to go drink in the bar, and that's when he got that driver licence from the policeman in Onslow. I don't know whether he went for the test or just get it like that.

He the only one allowed to go drink, not we fellas, and he not allowed to bring grog to the home. He used to go have a drink in the pub; he not allowed to bring any grog back and give it to the family. He could bring the grog, keep it himself; no one allowed to touch it. But we never used to touch it, we understand.

He had to talk with a lot of people to get that Citizen Right for his drink. He was the only one had a licence for drive the motor car, and licence go to the bar. All the other man around, all the Aborigine man, whatever good people, they all got Citizen Right. No woman; I never know any woman got the Citizen Right, only all the men. I think woman never used to worry about drink those days. We know — we used to drink at Christmas time — but from there, we never used to follow it like this people now, killing themselves. From there we used to go just with our own food and drink, whatever drink we make from the bush.

Getting his Citizen Rights, that's mean Jack was get mixed up with the whitefellas, and he think about whitefellas not classing him out. And he got all his family written in that Citizen Right, all the names what

From 1944 on the Natives' (Citizenship Rights) Act permitted certain Aboriginal people to be granted a form of citizenship. This required the person to be approved by a local magistrate (and after 1951 also a member of the local municipal council) as a literate, working, well-behaved member of society. They were given a certificate bearing their photo, and had to produce it when asked. On this certificate it was stated that this person was 'deemed to be no longer an Aborigine'. This insulting document was commonly referred to by Aborigines as a 'dog licence'. The degree of difficulty encountered in obtaining and keeping it depended on the attitudes of local authorities, and it was usually only of interest to people living near towns. Aborigines with this certificate were allowed to vote and to buy alcohol for their own use, but were forbidden to associate with any of their own people who might be called 'tribal'. Needless to say this was the restriction most often ignored. In the 1960s the 'dog licence' became redundant as most restrictions on Aborigines were lifted, and the Act was finally repealed in 1971.

wife and things. Well, he worked with that whitefella, now; they together. He allowed to come in just like the whitefella coming in to that drink. No more that used to be colour barring one another, the blackfellas not allowed to be there, only whitefellas. He find out he allowed to go there, and he reckon that's good for the family and him. And not only that, it might be good for the other family tribe. They all work together now, whitefellas and Aborigine. And more and more they was doing it.

You get that licence, you not supposed to mix with tribal people, that's what they said. But these fellas was mixed up with the tribal people — they couldn't part them out, because they're family. You got to stay in the family. He got nowhere to go — he can't get mixed up with the whitefella, unless he going to camp outside!

One night he went in jail in Onslow, my husband — he was drunk! He never been making trouble, just drunk. They put him in jail for a night. Policemen used to be good there, never used to chase the people. Ian Blair was there — he used to be a sergeant — and Dick Larsen, and one more, I can't remember his name. Only that night Jack got very drunk and they lock him up. Not only Jack — two, three people was in jail for a night. Those days nobody was fighting when they drunk. My husband used to come drunk and he never used to come up fight with us. He used to come straight to bed and finish. Wake up next morning he's good.

Ian Blair, he was good. My husband used to go see him all the time for little things what he need. I think it's the motor car parts, some of them; he had bits and pieces somewhere. When they drinking, they talk about all the things, and that's when we come to find out they a friend then. He never been rough-handle them people when he was a policeman, Ian Blair. He was a good bloke.

I used to drive the truck, but I had no licence. Because we want a job to be done and everybody got to drive the truck to get the job going. Out in the bush you don't get no policemen. When my husband used to go up to Roebourne — he might have a business; Dalgety used to be in Roebourne — he used to come do all the business, and we was keep working. I used to drive the truck and chop the tree down, and I know how to work the fence, put the fence up, bore the thing. We used to be good. They think I never been working all the man work, but I know. Yeah, everybody have to work, kids and all. Kids used to run the wire through the posts; the oldest ones about six to eight years old, they used to help. And that's why when they come to the whitefella job they know already, because they grow up in that job.

The gold help the dingo scalp and the kangaroo skin

If we run into dingo, we used to set the poison and trap.
That's bit of help, and that's a easy money: you get it
quick, you give it to the station and station sent that to the
shire office, and we used to get the money straightaway.
Dingo — those days there was lot.

They used to throw aerial bait in the river for killing
dingo, but that was dangerous for the kids. They put little
poison tablets in the tinned meat, and wrap them up in
paper just like lollies, and they drop it from the plane. If
they drop in the water and we go and drink that water,
that was dangerous for we fellas. You know, we make a
soak next to the pool, get clean water. Lucky we was
know them lollies one; we can see them in the water, and
my husband said, 'That's all the poison there, we not
allowed to drink that water.' We used to move, then, until
the river run again to wash them away. We was complain
then. But dingo never used to eat them, because they eat
kangaroo and sheep, fresh ones.

Summertime we used to get the kangaroo, not the
wintertime, only summertime. You only shoot the big
father one, old ones. Shoot all that, pack all the skins and
take them to Onslow and sell it and get all the stores and
the petrol and things.

If my husband's not there, we used to do night
shooting, all the women. We got a torch; we had the long

one, about six battery on the torch. We put it on top of the gun, and when the night-time come we used to go shooting now. We'd go to a long pool of water. We used to go out this side, shoot all the kangaroos this side, and when we come around the other side, shooting the other side now. We go have a sleep, little bit, then in the morning we have to come back, skin all the kangaroos and put it all heap and burn it all up. Used to work hard for that little bit of money in that kangaroo skin. And when we skin the kangaroo we might get a little bit of tail if he's a young kangaroo; we get the tail and we take it for meat, cook it.

Then we go back have a cup of tea or whatever we want, start pegging now. Might be thirty or forty kangaroo skins. We got to peg all that in the ground, flat out, to get it dry. It might be there for two or three days. Get it really dry so he won't smell. Then after, we pull them all out and bundle it up one on top of the other, flat. When Jack come back he'll tie them up then, tie them up tight and take them to Onslow and sell it. I couldn't remember how much we used to get, kangaroo, but not a lot.

Old Cranfield used to be in Onslow; he had a store there. We used to bring the skins to there, and he used to give us the money for the dingo scalps and kangaroo skins, and the stores and petrol to take out bush again. If we run out of petrol somewhere round the station, we got money to go and buy another lot of petrol and oil for the motor car. And Cranfield used to help us what food we got to get for the bush. Tinned meat and baked beans and spaghetti, all them things. And even the dry beans, those big white ones. We used to get lot of those in the bag. Those one are good for the bush, and split peas; we used to take that for cooking a kangaroo tail and things like that. They used to be nice. Cabbage, they used to have it in the packet, dry one, but you can't see them now. And we used to get a bag of salt.

If we kill a wild beef, we salt it, keep it salt in the bag. Every night we hang them up, and early in the morning before sun come up we go back and put it back in bag again. And when we want to cook it, we got to soak it in the water first, couple of pieces. I used to like it, but we're missing all them things now. Even the sheep, brisket part, and the shoulder and things, we used to salt it and keep it for long time; it used to be good.

We used to get gold, too; bits and pieces from every old mine. We used to go and fill up a jar. You could pick them up all outside — we never used to worry about digging, we just pick whatever we could find on the top. After big rain, that's the time we used to go, see all the gold laying there. We know all the mines, wherever we got to go. Some of the people like gold. Pat Ahmat used to be in Onslow; he used to buy gold from us. Those days, you know, gold was not very dear. Mrs Ahmat had a gold watch and gold teeth, and a gold ring, over them pieces now. But they only pay might be four hundred, five hundred dollar for jar like a big coffee mug those days.

We think we get enough, because we just worry about food more than anything else, and we never worry about the money hardly. We only wanted money for the petrol and things, and bit of food — might run out sugar or tea out in the station, you know — well we got to go buy something. And the gold help the dingo scalp and the kangaroo skin. That's all the money we used to get, no Social Security or children money — nothing. We had to work all the time.

8

BRINGING UP THE FAMILY IN
THE BUSH

We was just keep moving

Kooline Station, we been there four years, I think, till 1956. Then from Kooline these Red Hill people ring up; they want fencing done there now. That's '46 we went to Red Hill Station; that's same time that Monte Bello was bombing. We was there in Red Hill; we got the shake and things there, because Monte Bello not far from there. All the woman was in the camp; all the man was in the fence, working. We seen the plane, and we seen the light flashing near the sea. Then we hear the bang. We don't know what is it! And kids run under the truck when they hear the shake, you know. We thought sky was coming down. Oh, that was a real shock for us.

Station people know. They said, 'There's a bomb.' Red Hill boss, he said, 'That's a bomb, same that Maralinga.' We still don't know what is it, till 1980s. I went to court,

In the 1950s the British were permitted by the Australian government to explode nuclear devices on the Monte Bello Islands, about one hundred and sixty kilometres north of Onslow. One bomb was exploded in 1952, and two more in 1956, the flash and following mushroom cloud being observed by those onshore. Meanwhile, on the Australian mainland in 1953, two devices had been exploded at Emu Fields in South Australia, and between 1956 and 1963 there were seven further tests at Maralinga. Before these, the Aboriginal people in the district had been moved away, but security was lax and many people were subjected to radiation. There were years of official cover-ups, until in 1985 the Labor government set up a Royal Commission. This showed that many lives had been put at risk, and led to extensive compensation claims and health studies.

then, here in Karratha. They want to find out what happened those days, and I said, 'All the kids had a tummy ache. We had a sore eye from that bomb.'

My Marshall, oh, when he was four years old he was still drinking, and my mum come stay with me and she tell me, 'Why you feeding that big kid still? You're getting skinny.' I was little skinny woman! And she used to tell I got to give him a hiding. Marshall used to be like drink milk, milk all the time.

When the old truck broken down, we wanted a new one now. I think Pat Ahmat been order that new one, Morris truck. Little truck, not a big one. Those days everything was cheaper than this time, you know, all the motor car and things. And so we got the Morris, and we was working all round Red Hill Station then. We used to do quick work and then clear that car payment, never stop working all summer or wintertime. We was keep working all through, no holidays, till we clear all the debts. When we going to town, Onslow, we used to go pay all the debts then. Yeah, just paid it off.

I think nearly over a hundred people in the Onslow Reserve then — people from everywhere. Old people and young people and all the people that job going out; Horace Parker and them, they got pushed out from Mulga Downs, they went to Onslow, all of them. Got all the kids, little ones, and put them in the school there. My mum lived there long time, till she died. That's the time that houses was coming up then, when she died.

We was keep working in the fencing contract. We used to come visiting, two night camp, or sometime only one night camp. We used to just camp one side across the road from the Reserve, because too many people there. Visit my mum and all the aunties, you know. Old people from Red Hill and Yarraloola, they used to be all there. They all my husband's aunties; they Kurrama language people, Gordon Lockyer's mob, old people.

And one bloke come from Roebourne, Mick Durack his name. He one of Tootsie Daniel's family. He was there looking after the old people; he was in that new building then, and he used to help them old people all the time. It's a good life there. They had to settle down, you know, they got nowhere to go. They had to settle down in Onslow.

I see the proper Law old people in Yarraloola Station,

when they put Red Alexander through the Law. Because we are the mothers, we all had to come out there to put this boy through the Law. They got this boy, and next morning they bring him to where all the mums is, get all the bag of flour and things like that. Bring him in with us mob. After, all the ladies got to go away, and he got to stay by himself, only have all the mans there. Woman only come with the food or water: they not allowed to come up and stay with him there. 1956, that's when Monte Bello Islands was getting bombed. Marshall only four years old then. And that's the last proper Law I seen. From there, that's it, no more. When I come to Roebourne I seen different ways, they doing it different.

In Red Hill Station, we made a spinifex house for the fridge, because kerosene fridge got to have a windbreak. Anyway, we made a boughshed, nice one like a room. Then one of my cousin-brother went smoke cigarette inside the spinifex house, and he never shut the matches, he just light the cigarette and throw the matches away. There's a fire come up, burn everything inside, meat and all was in the fridge. Ooooh, that was the end of it. Goodbye for that fridge. He's still there now, standing! We had to order another one when we got money from the fencing. Lucky we used to make a little room like that for the fridge. We got our boughshed, camping one, it's a different one, and the fridge used to be one side.

Then from there we come back to Juna Downs again; one of the boss ask we fellas to manage the station. No

At the old mustering camp, 2002. Alice Smith and Nellie Jones built the cattle yards in 1957. Water is collected from a nearby night spring.
Front row: Alice Smith, her daughter Eva,
her daughter-in-law Helen, Georgina Connors and Norma James.
Alice's great-grandchildren are at the back.

proper job like these people working now. We was just keep moving. All the kids was growing up in the bush. Someone looking after, nanny's there, and she the one cooking the lunch or whatever she making for the workers.

We was looking after Juna Downs Station, and that's when I had Camis then, in 1957. Camis was born at Juna Downs Station, by the hill, not far from the station. He was a quicker one; only had a little bit of pain and when I went we had two old ladies and Amy and me, and Nelly Jones, and I had the baby eight o'clock in the night. Eight o'clock in the morning I was fixing a windmill! I was still bleeding! Because all the mans out mustering; no man there, and all the tank went dry. That wooden bolt come off from the pump, and those other ladies, they don't know how to fix it, only me. I had to, because none of them know how to do all the bolt thing, because I been working that long with the man jobs, I know how to work things out. I went up the ladder, climb up the windmill! I just get up and put the bolt in and that's it, and water come then. That was the funny one. Amy can tell you that, and they was worrying, too. I was worrying about we got no water, see. Anyway I went climb up, blood coming down my leg! Lucky only all the womans there. Any-way we fix that windmill, and they was give me lunch, get me back strong again!

Those days the women was strong,

Wyloo Station, 1955.
Left to right: Eva (Alice Smith's daughter), Inga and Marshall (Alice Smith's son). The small child is the station manager's daughter.

see, because we was living on the own food all the time. This time everybody eating takeaway food and everything. I used to run long way, too. I used to chase the kangaroo, when I was skinny. It was really good; I used to chase kangaroo and everything, and we used to walk twelve mile down, night-time when we coming back, twelve mile up back home.

And the old lady, Inga, she move out. She want to have a rest now, go her own way. She was midwife for all my kids. First she went to Wyloo Station. She was working there a little while in Wyloo Station. She had all the children there, Eva and Marshall and them. Then she moved to Onslow then, because no one allowed to be in Wyloo Station, and she was living in the Reserve.

You can't have a argue with the doctors

When I was pregnant with Charlie, my husband was working Red Hill Station again. It was really hot there, and that's why he want us to go and stay in Onslow for a while till the baby's out. Camis was sick, he had a tummy trouble. And so my husband tell me, 'You might as well stay in Onslow for a while, have the baby and things.' And so I stayed there — my mother was alive then, we were staying in the Reserve. My Camis, he was two years old. I tell him not to drink milk now, because I got no more milk.

But if he walking around, he used to find another kid drinking their mum's milk, he used to go drag them away and he put himself in! Oh jingoes — he used to be terrible!

I had to have the baby in the hospital. I was upset but I got nowhere to go, see, because no Onslow people know how to help the woman with having a baby. Mum not allowed to be helping daughter, in Aborigine way, or my own aunty, they not allowed to be there. I don't know how they used to do it, Thaianyji* people. Before the whitefella come round they got to have a baby out in the bush. In the hospital it was really different way. You know, those days we was scared about the whitefella. I had four kids in the bush, and this number five in the hospital — ooh, God!

And anyway when I come to the hospital, I seen the doctor standing — man! That man come from Port Hedland. We never have a man in the bush, Aborigine people. In the bush nobody can tell you what to do, you know yourself whatever things you got to do. Anyway I had this baby there, and I just take it what they want me to do. Strange! Lying down, in the bed! I already had four; this was the number five one, so I know what I'm doing, but you can't have a argue with the doctors, you know. When you're in the hospital you got someone telling you what to do.

Cord, that's wrong for me, in the hospital, because we do it a different way. We don't cut that cord from the baby till everything out. When everything out clean, then we cut it, and we bury that thing in the hole where the baby been born. Dig a hole there and bury it there. I was a little bit upset, but I got to take it what they do, you can't do nothing. Can't tell them to bury it in the ground. I don't know what they done. I don't know. And they cut the cord only short one, and they tie him up with the string then.

I stayed there one week in the hospital; they make you stay in bed. That strange for me, because when we have a baby out in the bush, we don't lay down in bed, we walk round straightaway doing something. Working. But in the hospital you had to stay in bed, somebody got to work for you.

Amy was there in Onslow too. She minded my kids, and my mother and my nieces. They all stayed in the Reserve. Camis was a little boy, he used to go over the fence fishing. Hospital was near the beach, and when I used to sit out on the verandah I'd see that little boy going to the sea now, fishing. Standing in the sea fishing with a little stick!

He used to be clever kid, too, that Camis. He used to see something in the dream, you know. He used to get up in the morning and tell us, 'I seen so-and-so man coming today. He'll be here today.' He'll tell us before anybody can ring up or we know somebody coming. He just see it in the dream, and when we used to hear it, that man is coming today. I don't know whether he still like that now. He might be lost all that now.

After I had Charlie, we was fencing there, out in the

bush. One of the Welfare people come see me about that Child Endowment. They was looking for us, come to Red Hill Station, and Red Hill Station people tell him where to go find us out in the bush. They ask me whether I getting it and I said, 'No, we never get any extra money, just getting the money from the fence, what we do.' I don't know whether they travel to all the stations; I only know they come to us at the fencing camp, and they do all the paperwork there then. We were scary, because Welfare people the one been taking all the kids away from the land. I was little bit worried why they coming. We just worried about they might pick up something to tell on us, you know. We weren't worried about them taking the kids away no more, because lot of kids was in Onslow then — they never been taken away, they schooling there. Yeah, pretty safe, we know.

Every fortnight we go back, or station manager used to bring a killer from the station, sheep, live one, to the bush, and that's the time he bring the mail then, and then they handed over to us whatever cheque. We used to get Child Endowment cheque every month, I think. If we out fencing or something we pick up the mail whenever we finish. We had no bank account. When we got a cheque we used to go to Onslow to get the food and get the clothes and things for the kids, and we used to change it in the shop. I only just was crossing it first, and give it to the storekeeper and he give me the cash and I buy clothes and things for the kids, whatever they need. And whatever left over, we used to get more food to take out bush again. It was a good help then.

I can sign my name now. I learn a little bit later when I was in Juna Downs Station; Mrs Herbert teach me to sign my own name. I used to do it every day till I pick up properly, you know. I was good then, sign my own name. And when I come to change that cheque in Wittenoom, I used to come change it there in the shop then. And when they see that cheque got my name from the Welfare, and he seen my writing in the bottom, they know I'm really me. That's what they used to do.

Jack Smith used to be really good witchdoctor

We always been handling all the bush medicine and the bush powder and things like that. They get sick, they get a flu, we get the bush medicine. When a baby is sick, or big kids, mother know what to do, because we got the things the old people tell us. When he high temperature, get this medicine. When he got flu, get that medicine, and when he got sore eyes, get that medicine. Well, we used to use that and kids used to be better straightaway. We got the medicine ready all the time there, in a basin or something. When I was a kid they had all that wooden yandy dish; old days the hard one. When I got my kids, different way, I had all them basin and plate and things now, and we could boil the water in a bucket.

We used to get that *minjariti* — that's the medicine like a rubbing Vicks. You get the green leaf, you break it up, put it in the bed and put a sheet over the top, and then you lie down, cover up so that steam could come up everywhere there, when you've got a flu. You could smell all that stuff now — it's nice, that one. When you've got a flu, bad one, it used to be good. And for a flu, we used to go walk get the wild honey, put him in a cup and make it like a cool drink, you know, mix it with the water, and the little one can drink and soften it inside. And when he coughing, he bring it all up.

For very high temperature, we used to get that bark from the cork tree, burn him black, and we used to put like a powder, make him black all over, to keep it cool. And then little one used to go to sleep, and he wake up really good now; now more sick. And kangaroo meat, we used to cook it on top of the coals, specially the liver and a little bit of fat; that's the main one for the kids sick. They eat that little bit, and that make it good inside, and they fix it properly. When you've got a headache you have to get another stuff, and keep it cold all the time when your head ache. Put a rag or something that'll tie it on, till you get through all them things. If you really bad we have a witchdoctor.

My husband, Jack Smith, used to be really good witchdoctor. He learn that from his old stepfather, Aborigine one, Johnny. He used to be clever, too, that old man. You wouldn't believe me, if I tell you how Jack been

Outcamp, Cheela Plain, Wyloo, 1934.

lifing all the sick people. He's only the one been like that.

Two ladies was very, very sick. Both of them had a baby, same day; Leary and Joyce. When they had a baby they was both very sick, and my husband fixed this one lady first in our camp, and the other lot been ring him up from Rocklea Station. We was in the outcamp, and our nephew come tell him, 'You got to come quick, down station now, because one lady's going off there; she's keep running away from the people, and people don't know what to do with her. And the new baby there.' Anyway, my husband went then, he went back there and see her. She reckon it's the emu singing out there on the ground and this turkey here, and that's why she took off everywhere, running long way. People got to chase her, she was going off. And my husband come, seeing her, and you won't believe me, because you got different ways. He can see what's going on about her head, he see it right through like x-ray, and he reckon it's just like a fan doing it in her head, inside, and that's why she running around. And he take that thing out, and this lady is good then, nothing wrong with her. She's alive today now, and she will tell you the same story, too.

Then that little one, Charlie, he had that pneumonia, and we bring him to Wittenoom hospital. All the trouble we had, coming up that night — big rain, from Juna Downs to Wittenoom Gorge. We found a kangaroo in the road, something put the kangaroo in the rain; the kangaroo sitting front of the motor car. And someone shoot it, kill him, and this old lady made a fire and cooked the little bit of liver and a little bit of kangaroo fat. I was sitting in the car, because with this little one's high temperature I didn't want to get in the rain. And she come up telling me, 'Give this to little boy, because it going to fix him.' It did, and kid was nothing wrong when he come to Wittenoom hospital. We take him to the doctor, doctor said he's all right now, nothing wrong with him. We just come up and go back again, then! He was all right!

It's the funniest thing that kangaroo been in the road. Somebody been put it in the road to help the little one. But my husband know what it is, because he know everything how this thing working, see. He can see them in the dream, then he tell us in the morning what's been happening that night, and we know he's telling the truth.

Once we was at Cheela Plain in Wyloo Station and Nelson Hughes brought Friday Smith to my husband, from Roebourne. That old man is stranger; we don't know him. We heard about him, but we never knew the family. Nelson, because he was the son-in-law belong to that Friday Smith, he bring him down there, because Jack Smith was cousin-brother for Nelson. Every time when the full moon come and the sea come up full tide, this old fella's tummy grow right up like a big balloon. He go hospital, doctor can't find out what's wrong with that old fella. They try everything, couldn't find anything. Nelson bring him all the way to Cheela Plain, and he tell my husband the old fella sick. All right, my husband want to see him now.

The witchdoctor's got a special thing, a *maban*, we call it. He sent it to that sick man, and this sick man sitting there. And he goes through his body, find out what's going on. And he go right to what's wrong, and my husband smell that one, and he reckon it smelling like the sea. All right, now he knows what he got — he got caught. One man in Roebourne used to be clever, killing all the people — old Possum. Old people, magic people, they get a stingray tail, they keep that one, and use it for bad things. They put some hair belong to the old fella in the ground, and in the wet ground they put that stingray thing, and all the salt going to come up to that man's body then. That's how he got sick.

The spirit we got inside our body, that's the spirit they're using for magic. Then my husband got his special spirit, magic one — he get this old fella's spirit, take him away from his body, take him in the Dreamtime, get it fixed there. He took his spirit — Jack's spirit gone too — took him to a special place where he got, fixed this old fella up. And anyway, they bring his spirit back, put it back on the old fella — old fella was working with us building a yard now! He was good! I think that was 1957. He was helping us fixing that Cheela Plain cattle yard. We brought him back to Roebourne after one month, and that old fella went back to work again. He used to work for Telecom people; he got that job back, he went another twenty and thirty years nothing wrong. That old fella was working right up 1985. I think he died when he was old age. He used to give money to my husband, after what he done. He was really good, and he used to look after us when we come here, that old fella now. See, he used to think about his life all the time — he wouldn't have been alive.

Same thing happen when we was in Mulga Downs, and this call from Roebourne, urgent telegram come to Mulga Downs Station. We was out bush, right up near other side of the highway going to Newman. We was there, and we seen the plane coming; the boss come to us. What's wrong now? And he come along, tell, 'Jack, you've got urgent telegram from Roebourne. They want you there very quick.' Because old Fred Hicks, Kenny Hicks' father, he was in the hospital, and doctor don't know what happen. He couldn't breathe, and things like that; something wrong with the foot. Same thing happened, that stingray stuff now. When Jack come, they went and bring him back from the hospital, and he had a look, and he clean everything up. He was good right up to 1989; old age again, Fred Hicks died. That's how clever Jack used to be. Now this time, finish; no more clever people we got now. We only got to go to the hospital all the time.

My husband didn't give the maban to any of the boys. *Juna*, that's the spirits, they come up all the time — night-time — visit him all the time, and want to have to fight him in secret way in the bush. And that's why he didn't wanted to give the maban to my boys. If he give the maban on his boys, well somebody else from other country will keep come. Too dangerous. He wanted their life to be differenter than him, that's why he didn't wanted it. Because he always been fight all the time in the bush. That spirit can kill you too, fighting amongst theirself, but lot of people don't know that. Lots of dangerous things. He didn't wanted to pass to the boys, because it'd be danger. When he gone, well boys'll be no danger then, it'll be okay, see.

When we was in Kooline working, he got hurt when he come down in the spirit, you know. He was paralysed one side, then he went to Onslow hospital, and he got fixed up that time. I think it was fifty-something, between '42 and '46. He was going good for a while then. Later, when he getting the old age, that stroke come there now. When he got the stroke, that was that place he got hurt before.

Jack Smith always had to fight out in the bush. We don't see that, only himself; he used to do it. He used to tell us when we having tea or lunch, he go out. He don't say for what, he go out camping by himself. That's when you know he's fighting in the spirit, and he killing lot of people too, in the spirit. That's what they call it, just like a warrior.

And he could life a lot of old people. Leary Delaporte, Joyce Injie, Friday Smith from Roebourne, Fred Hicks from Roebourne. They was dying, you know. The doctors don't know what happen; that's because juna man been take them like that. They used to send an urgent telegram from Mulga Downs to tell him to come down and see them. All of them was life, every one of them.

The first kid mine going to Perth Hospital

For a while we was working in Brockman Station, near Hamersley, helping old Jack Edney. I was pregnant then. We come to Hamersley Station in the weekend, and I feel the pain then, and then they rushed me into hospital to Wittenoom. Doctor Oxer was the doctor then; he was a good doctor. Same sort of treatment I had before, but I was little bit used to now. I know what they going to do with me.

Then 1961 I had Nina there and I was staying in the

hospital. This was the races time, Wittenoom races. They let me out with the baby and we went back to Hamersley just for a couple of weeks. We wanted to go pick the old lady up, but we got in the rain and the motor car got in the bog. And this baby got sick, Nina — she had that meningitis — and we had to rush back to the hospital again, put her on the plane. Nurse had to go with her, and I was crying, going mad. That's the first kid mine going to Perth Hospital. Oh, we went mad, all the kids was crying, all the big brothers. Everybody was crying, that baby gone. Because those days they never let the mum to go with the baby. Now you allowed to go, take your baby, but those days not. Nurse had to take her. They put her on the bottle then, and they give me the tablet to stop the milk.

She was away for five weeks, and we got no news. We wouldn't know whether the baby's okay or what. You just put that baby on the plane and you wouldn't know what's going on. Five weeks is long time. But you got no one to help you. And Jack Edney's an old-timer, you know, he don't know nothing about kids! And the boss people in the station — it was Lang Hancock. He's the one boss Hamersley and Mulga Downs, see. Lang Hancock used to never help Aborigine people; he was greedy for money.

There was no Welfare in Wittenoom; they used to come from Roebourne. Then Frank Dwyer*, I think, that was the Welfare in Roebourne, he come let us know that baby coming back. Me and him meet the baby at Wittenoom airport then. She was okay; no more problem. She was good, but she never been walking till eighteen months. She had all the needles — you could see all the lumps on her back. She was very sick, Nina. Lucky she got to the doctor. Doctor Oxer was there. He said, 'Lucky this girl never brain damaged' or something; paralysed. Lot of people get brain damaged with that meningitis.

Old Inga was in Onslow. They had a tent in the Reserve. They had them cyclone bed, that hard one. And when it start raining and lightning striking everywhere, next thing when they coming into the tent, lightning strike right where the tent is. And one old lady, Daisy Cox — Leary Delaporte's mum — her hair went yellow like an orange. It got burnt with that lightning. The other lady got kicked over — thrown over long way, get like getting blown up. And that one Inga is died. She was sort of buried underneath the sand. It was really bad, and everybody was screaming there, they reckon. She's in Onslow cemetery too, same as my mum and my aunty and uncle. That was a terrible one, really bad.

Nina was still crawling when Andrew was born, in Wittenoom again. Andrew was crawling, the young brother born in 1962, and Nina was crawling. You think they was twins then. I used to put them in the pram, both of them. I had three in Wittenoom: Nina, Andrew and Susan; those three belong to Wittenoom. So then I had eight kids.

Then the money changed. We knew the old one: one

shilling, two bob, five bob. Big one five bob we used to have. Ten bob, and one pound. One pound note is a green note. We had a little bit of trouble with the new money, and then we got used to them. Somebody show my husband, and he come up show us, and we pick up from there then. Because ten cents is same as a shilling, see. They only call them ten cents. And that twenty cents is same as the two bob. They only just calling different way. And this fifty cents, that's a five bob! One pound is two dollar. This is dollar, this is dollar — when we put it together this is only one pound! They got the five cents — that's the sixpence we use, but that threepence, that the littlest one, that one never come, I don't know what happen. And penny, we used to have, them big ones; penny, but they had that little one, two cents and one cent. And that ten dollar is a five pound for us, used to be. It's funny.

When we was doing the contract we used to go to Wittenoom for stores. In the shop we would just follow the pictures to know what everything was. But we know the prices; somebody used to teach us. Mrs Corrigan, and her sister Barbara Reynolds, they used to be doing the same contract working out in the bush; they used to show us all the prices, and then I know all the time then, when I come to the new money.

9

SCHOOLING FOR THE FAMILY

They can read that paper for us

When the Welfare's turned good, they come and explain to people now. They come up tell us about school when we were still in the bush. So we sent three kids: Marshall, Eva and Gladys. They went to Onslow first; that was about '49* they went there, schooling. Eva and Gladys was nine, they both, and Marshall was seven, when they first start the school. They was little bit older than age for that school. Anyway, we put them in Onslow; someone been looking after them there for us — I think she used to be a Welfare lady*. We used to leave the kids for one year. We trust that white lady, one of the friend belong to us. Ian Blair, that's the policeman, used to help that lady to look after these kids.

They only had one school for the white kids, no separate one, and when Aborigine kids come, well, they had to put them mixed up. My kids never had a problem. They had to go. They was sad for a while, specially

Marshall. He was only seven years old then. He was sad for a while, and then he was getting good; that lady, Mrs Rooney, was there looking after them. She used to get the clothes for them, from the Welfare, I think.

They been there about one or two years with that lady, and we was in Juna Downs then, looking after Juna Downs Station. We was mustering all the brumbies and the horses and the cattle. Oh, we was sad for a while, but we get used and used, now*; we feeling they did do the right thing.

Geoff Herbert that give us the job to look after Juna Downs, he had Cane River Station. He had two stations, and they were still looking after the sheep station, because Cane River had sheep. That's why he want we fellas to look after this one; Juna Downs only had horse and cattle. One of his kids, Matt Herbert, same age my kids, they schooling in Onslow too. When they got two-week holiday, they used to go and pick the kids up, bring them holiday there. They never bring them to us, because too far away from Onslow to there. They used to keep them and put them back in the school. He was good. We was in Juna Downs all around there and mustering cattle and wild brumbies, and they used to come Christmas holiday, someone bring them. Christmas holiday, that's all.

Yes, those three went, and Des, he wanted to stay working; he's the oldest in the family. He didn't wanted to go school with the other kids. We had him doing the schooling there, bush one. We had a whitefella friend there in Cowra; he like kids, and he used to teach Des.

Stockyards built by Jack Smith at Coppin Pool, Juna Downs Station.

That was good, too, help us read a lot of things, you know. After work he used to go down there to see him and that old fella been teaching him to read and write. Des never been to school.

When the kids come home, notice change now. They used to show all the thing what they doing over there, and we understand properly then; they doing a good thing. Yeah, they taught us how the school going, how they can read that paper for us, or whatever letter we getting from friends. They read it for us, and that's good. And from there, that lady gone now. They got nowhere to go back to school.

Christmas holiday they bring them and we move to

Hamersley then; we was work in Hamersley, cattle mustering. We was keep moving, you know, looking for money wherever the work. We took them away for Christmas holiday and then we had them at Mulga Downs and they was missing six months, now — they got to go back to school again. All right, this Welfare come up — Mr Parker — ask we fellas could we find somebody to keep them kids in Roebourne for six months in schooling, till we find a proper place to settle down. And them kids say, 'Yes, we want to go school.'

Lot of Aborigine people used to have a camp in Roebourne in the river near the hostel, and the other lot in the Reserve. One old lady* — Mibben Low and his family, one of our relation — we know them all the time, friends. They was living this edge of the river with a tin house, little one, near the school. Anyway they come up there, stay there for six months. We was on Mulga Downs Station then, working; we was doing fencing and sheep yard and oh, everything there. Right up the other side of Newman Highway, right up to the marsh there, we was doing all the fencing. We was on Mulga Downs all the time until 1967.

We put them in Nullagine Mission

Then we find out that the Nullagine Mission is the home for schooling for all them through here. So after six months we bring them back to Mulga Downs for two-week holiday, then we put them in Nullagine Mission now: Marshall, Eva and Gladys, them three. And Des was working with us. We took them down there, we got to meet the boss, you know, the headmaster and things like that. George Stevens, he's the one got the Nullagine Hostel, and they was there 1961*, '62, '63. Sixty-four* they finish up there. School and hostel separate. Hostel just for the kids that are going to school — no mums, you know. They been four years there, in Nullagine, and they made all the friends — they was happy there. Lot of Aborigine children was in the hostel; one of the young Aborigine lady was looking after the kids there. Two-week holiday they used to come back, and Christmas holiday, to Mulga Downs. All the little ones, we had them all in Mulga Downs.

Old Billy Dunn is a Nyiyaparli man*. He was got a gold mine somewhere there, and every Friday he used to come in to Nullagine and pick them kids up, because he had a girlfriend working in the hostel. Maureen, her name, and Billy Dunn come pick the girlfriend and pick three kids belong to us, take them for weekend every time. They used to go out bush then; Friday, Saturday, they was camping out, and Sunday afternoon they used to come back. That was good; they was like it. That's the way they got the language, learning Aborigine way belong to there now. They was doing it good there. Yeah, when Marshall come back he talk Nyiyaparli*!

Yeah, in Nullagine they all mixed up: they had

Nyiyaparli and Kariyarra and Nyamal and everything there, and Jigalong mob was there too. My kids had Banyjima ways from home, from my place, and they learn other lot of language there. And how they cooking and things like that. There's lot of people used to camp in the river, all them people.

George Stevens is a Christian man. They used to have a church every Sunday, and they used to read Bible and thing. When they come back they had a Bible themself then. They had all the picture of the Jesus and all them things.

We had that ourself, in the tribal way. They talk about everything — well, we got that same, Aborigine people. But *some* Aborigine people don't know Jesus, and that's how they went off, you know. But we know all the time; my mum and dad used to be like that. No swearing and things like that, you know. You not allowed to steal things, you not allowed to walk into anybody's house even if nobody home. All them things — we had all that. When this whitefella Christian life come up to us, we know all the time. But this people here, Roebourne, I ask them, but they don't know Jesus when they was by themself before the whitefella come. And that's the way they still lost now, don't know where they going.

When the kids come up read us the Bible, you know, all the words they reading the same as our Aborigine ways. Everything we talk about, same. That whitefella way Christian and blackfella way Christian — they all same, where I come from. And that's the way we just leave it to that, the kids learning good.

They go back bush all the time for holiday. Oh, they think they is a big shot when they come back. Read everything, and school work; do all the school work teaching us, now! We got somebody there to tell us what's going on then. When we used to get a letter, you know, we got to wait for some of the whitefellas to come up and read it for us. Station boss, sometime. Now when we got them, we right. They was good!

They like the old ways. They like that fire they used to make. When we used to make big cooking fire, the whole lot, they used to make a little own one, after they miss all that when they was in the school. They got to cook it themself — little damper, meat not in the grill, just top of the coal they put it on. And they cook it like that. They used to have a little fruit tin, billycans, boil the tea for themself. They used to be like it. Chop the meat with a knife themself. When they finished, sometimes they tell us, 'We go looking for food now; bush food.' They used to go out with the jeep, looking for all the food, with the box. Wild orange, and wild passionfruit, and wild onions — them little ones in the ground. They used to go hunting.

They do both way now. They still doing it now, but most of the time they want to go bush all the time. Long as they still come back to us, we got to teach them our way, and when they in the school they pick up from the whitefella way. And when they come back to us, we use both way, whitefella and Aborigine way.

When they come back home, they never lost that language. Language got to be there too, you know; that's the main part. If they lose whatever language we talking, only talk whitefella way — well they lost. And that's why we had to keep them kids back, to keep it in home, so we teach our language, and they learn about whitefella way in the school. When they come back they got to talk our own language.

When Wirrianna Hostel was opening in Roebourne, Marshall and Eva come stop with Dave Stevens. They was in the tin house there, back of Tsakalos' garage, where that fire engine now standing*, in 1965. Sixty-six, that hostel opened then, and all the young ones come up now; mine and Amy's. They all was in the hostel. Camis, Kensey and Charlie and Nina and Roy. Five of them come to the hostel.

Eva finished: 1964 she was turned fifteen, and she didn't wanted to go high school, and so she put in for job in the hostel, looking after the children. She was staying in the hostel then, and that was good. And Gladys put in for job in Marble Bar hostel; she was working in Marble Bar then with George Stevens — that's that man at Nullagine Mission. He moved to that hostel, and his son moved to Roebourne Hostel, Dave Stevens. And so these two girls think one got to work in other hostel and this one got to work here. They arrange themselves, you know, and Marshall only the one going to school in Roebourne then.

Marshall was still going to school, then he went to high school one year, in Applecross in Perth. That's all he went, only one year high school, because those days we had no government money covered the costs, and we only in that contract. Contract people, you don't get money straightaway, you got to put the fence three or four mile before you get all the money. And that's why we just let him one year Perth and that's it. Yeah, put him in the plane all the time.

Only just the whitefella way they learn about in the hostel, because no Aborigine people was running the hostel. When they get that Aborigine girls was working there, Rosie Cheedie and my daughter Eva, and Welfare woman used to be there, Welfare used to ask Eva and Rosie when they going out, lunch hour, they'll have to teach them Aborigine way how they go bush; how they're hunting things — wild honey or whatever food they're getting. And they was bit better then, when they had couple of Aborigine ladies there. Mr and Mrs Stevens used to be really good; they understand about the Aborigine way. You know, they let them two girls to do it Aborigine way, teach them kids. Teach their kids, too, Ruth Stevens and them.

10

MOVING TOWARDS TOWN

I never came here to settle down

When we finish Mulga Downs fencing, the station people sent a letter to us could we come up help them mustering wild cattle in the wild country round back of Pyramid, back of Woodbrook and back of Karratha Station; sheep country, right back to Fortescue. The station people didn't wanted the wild cattle knocking all the fence down. Contract work — own contract. Might be Pyramid Station first, and then go to Cooyapooya, and from Cooyapooya to Cherratta, all around Karratha, right back to Fortescue roadhouse. All the wild cattle was running there. We just got the money from the cattle, the stations don't pay us.

Before we get the money, we got to put that cattle in the truck. We used to come up to Roebourne, and if we got no money when we here, Dalgety's used to give us a load of tucker for a month. When the cattle truck gone, and the cattle sold, they'll take a half of the money and give us half of the money. Half of the money pay for the truck, that's the way we used to work out. It's hard, though, very hard; night and day they used to work in the cattle mustering. There might be no yard; then you've got to shepherd the cattle all night.

We had our own horses. We had started from Rocklea, Wyloo all around; we had them horses, and horses got to move wherever we moving. We leave the horses in Hamersley when we coming to Mulga Downs. When we finish, we go and pick the horses, and the cattle mustering start near here, and we bring all the horses back here.

That's when I first came to Roebourne, but never came here to settle down, I just came here to do all the mustering. Dalgety's was a good store then; Alec Barnett used to be there. That's the boss used to be running that shop. He helped people. We got no money, we get food from there — take all the tucker or petrol or whatever is, get it through him. And when we truck the cattle, then we pay back. That's the way we used to work. Even the gun, bullets, or whatever we need. He was really good bloke, he help anybody.

You can't have a baby in the bush

When I had the last baby, Angus, I was still working fencing and all them things. Angus was born on Pyramid Station, in the bush, in 1967. I don't want to come in the hospital; I was happy have it there, bush. I had nobody to boss me round then! I was out in the sand. When you come to the hospital, well this doctor tell you to do this and do that. Man doctor, used to be: Doctor Manton. That's why I didn't wanted to come to the hospital. When you're bush, you know what to do yourself, specially the Aborigine people. We know what to do ourself in our culture way. I just sit down, midwife sitting down there, all she do holding the pain or something like that, don't tell me what I got to do. I got to do it myself. When the baby out, the midwife do something about the baby. And when everything over, they just cut it, bury the baby bag, clean the baby, and that's it. I had three ladies there: Amy, and Elsie Tucker, and Allie* Tucker's mother, too. He was a fat baby, too; he was ten pound when he born. Ah, he was a big baby, that Angus!

My husband was doing fencing at the racecourse in Hedland*. I been two days there, and when he come back he ask me, 'What about I go and leave you one week in the hospital and get strong, you know? Baby get strong.' And I was happy then when I come to Roebourne Hospital. Have a little bit of rest. If I'm out, well I work all the time. After two days, when I come to the hospital they weigh it. He was nine pound then, after two days.

And when I come to Roebourne Hospital, those nurses never believe me I had it in the bush. They said, 'Where you had the baby?'

'I had it in the bush.'

'You can't be,' one of the nurse say, 'you can't have a baby in the bush. No one allowed to have a baby in the bush!'

'Yeah, I had the baby in the bush.'

When he get born he was in the sand, full of sand, and they don't know whether I telling lie or telling the truth. But the baby always born in the sand, and they got to clean it after, you know. Wipe out the face. We got to find a nice soft sand.

Murray Stove's wife, Mrs Stove, she was the matron working there, and she come along now, because she's olden-day lady — Mount Welcome Station manager's wife. She tell all the girls, 'You got to believe Alice, because the Aborigine people had the baby before the hospital come up here. They belong to here. They have a baby wherever they want to have a baby. They don't have a hospital like we fellas. They have it and they just clean it and walk around straightaway. They don't lay in bed like we fellas!' Oh, make them look now, young girls, you know. They thought Aborigine people don't have it in the bush! Yes, it's the young sisters, they didn't know that.

Those days all the Roebourne Aboriginal people used to have their babies in the hospital. They lost the old ways when they come and live in that Reserve; that's when everything change. And most of the lady used to work in the hospital too, cooking and doing all the washing and things, and they find out hospital was good. Well they want to have the baby in the hospital then, all the young one. When you've got no one to look after you, it must be some danger then, for the young mothers. You'll have to go to the hospital then.

I just been there one week. My husband was doing the fence at Roebourne racecourse by then; he's the one put that fence around the racecourse. He used to come and see me, and Amy was in the Reserve then, looking after the kids, and my daughter-in-law Dinah. She was with us then, but she never was living with my son; we was keeping it separate for a while till the time come ready that they get married. She was looking after the kids. They were staying there for a while with the relation, you know. They used to live with them fellas for little while.

We got a little bit of place, now

Then when I out of the hospital we were going back bush again. We was doing cattle mustering round the back, all the wild ones, because Murray Stove and them, they didn't wanted all the wild cattle breaking the fence, you know. They got a lot of sheep.

Then Cherratta Station, they had no fences. They had sheep and horses there, and when we finish cattle mustering, they ask we fellas to put the fence up now, boundary and things. Coppin Dale had no money in Cherratta Station to pay all the fencing job, and so he think, 'We'll give you a little bit of land near Cherratta.' Old Coppin Dale and them, they belong to this land. So Cherratta give us a little bit of lease on Munni Munni Creek, top end of Cherratta. We got a little bit of place now, leasing it. That's what happened. And so we leave all the horses there then. That's was really good, worked out for the horses too. And a few cattle we bought it from Yalleen, two hundred cow. We put it in that area now, to breed. They was trucking some away, but when the big drought come, some of them died, you know — no feed. And few cattle still there. Then we settle down near Roebourne then, but we still had the horses and the cattle there. They're bush horses. They got their own food, they was always like that. You look after the horse when they sick, you know, you don't let them go till he get better. When they better they could let them back in the paddock again. That good for them too, you know, running round.

Roebourne Reserve was really good then, because no grog those days. Coppin Dale and some other people, they was the boss for all the people. Two women got to work, clean the laundry and the woman toilet; two man got to clean that man toilet and keep it clean. They was really good there. All the people was good. Clean, and all the kids used to go to school, and they used to come to the cafe and have lunch there, from the school. Kids used to walk to school from across the river.

They had houses, them Welfare houses, government people used to put it in the Reserve. Tin houses, just like a little portable house. Some got two rooms, some got three bedroom, and a kitchen in the one place, and dining room and everything. Too little for a big family, but they used to put up with it; they used to put a boughshed for extra one. They used to have a little windmill working there, pumping the water.

It was pretty strict. No kids allowed to be stay away from school, they used to come to school all the time. King and Coppin Dale and Churnside and Kenny Gerald's father, Jerry, and Peter Jacob, and Long Mack. That's all the old people, was the good people. They had everything working good. And Barbara Churnside's father, Milton Churnside, he's another one.

They used to kill a bullock in the slaughter yard near the pipeline. They used to kill the bullock and the pigs and the sheep. Tsakalos and Gig Heald, they was the butcher, and Barbara Churnside's father was a butcher, and Churnside himself, he used to be butchering, and Coppin Dale. They used to work there, and there was a butcher shop with an underground room to keep all the meat.

We used to get everything from the Dalgety's now, and he's the one help us do all the cattle mustering and things. When we first come, we don't know nobody here, and that old Gig Heald, he used to give us a part for the motor car too. He was a nice old bloke, but his son died in the accident, near Pyramid. That was really sad. The old fella didn't wanted to keep that Land Rover, and he give it to my husband. We got the same sort of Land Rover like that one, and they just tow it out of the road, take it between the snakewoods, and he tell my husband he could have all the parts from there, because he didn't wanted to see it.

They used to have a couple of whitefellas that were running round buying the grog, you know, and give it to the people in the Reserve because they want a woman, or something like that. They used to supply that thing. But we used to come in from bush, only my husband used to drink, and he never used to bring it. Sometime he used to get bottle of whisky and a bottle of wine — the flat bottle — and he used to bring them bush. That's just for when I'm tired; he used to give me one little glass in the water, and drink it and go to sleep. That's all. We might be have it two months before we finish the bottle, you know. Just taking little bit every time tired, working all day.

Then Mount Welcome mob — Murray Stove used to be there — he asked we fellas to put a fence up, because the train line going up then. We were staying in the shearing shed, and we put fence in the train line, between Karratha Station and Mount Welcome boundary, all them fence on the side of the main road. We put all that, and all the sheep yards there. That was 1969.

We was in Cheeditha, the old shearing shed; Murray Stove give us the place to stay there. He was good. He used to give us the sheep — killer, you know — every Saturday. Water and everything there. No power, but we had a lamp, and most of the night we used to sit in the camp fire. We allowed to make a fire around the back.

There was me, Amy, and Dinah, my daughter-in-law. We was three there. And some people used to visit us there, from Onslow. My sister's family, they used to come stay there for holiday. Murray Stove wouldn't mind family coming up there.

Shearing time they used to shear the sheep there and we used to help them, shearing. You know, clean all the rubbish out for them. And we used to have a lot of sheep tail; shearing time they chopped the tail off. They used to fill the bag and give it to us. We like that one, cook it Aborigine way in the flame. Clean it properly, it's nice. Good tucker, we used to be like it.

My youngest son, Angus, he used to have the asthma. One night when he only about two years old, middle of the night we had to walk all the way from shearing shed to the hospital. We only got one motor car; when they're out working, all the boys, then we was just all walking round. And I had to walk all the way to the hospital with the little one sick. This time you've got someone always running round to the camp, but those days no one was helping. We had a hard time.

The big kids was in the hostel. Every Friday night they used to come back to the woolshed. Sunday night we bring them back to the hostel then. Monday they're schooling. They was good; they used to the hostel. Mr and Mrs Stevens really good. They had four children themself: Ruth and John, Phillip and Paul.

11

LIVING IN ROEBOURNE

Me and him might as well be separate

Then my husband and I used to have argument all the time, how he missing all the time, not coming home. We was working for Murray Stove, living in that old Cheeditha woolshed then, and he used to go out to the pub and stay all night right up to next morning. Come back in the morning, just straight to the work. Then I tell him that me and him might as well be separate, you know; no fighting. 'If you want to go with a girlfriend, well you got free to go now, see. I'm out of the trouble. All I want, to look after the kids going to school.' I had a row with him couple of time but he never take any notice to me.

But I work different way now, and I ask him to get a house in town then. And he put in for house then, so we get that house in Sherlock Street. And the girlfriend belong to him, she come to the house — she was looking for him — and me and Amy was sitting there with the kids. She was drunk. And I walked to the gate, and that lady homemaker across the road, Mrs Morris, she ran out, and she know what was going on, because she know what's going on in the pub, see. She used to work in the pub. Anyway she run, and she tell me, 'Ring the police first,' and she run grab me, put me back in the house. And policeman come. He ask what the trouble and I tell him she looking for husband mine. So he put her in the 'cocky cage', drunken woman.

And from that we was good one week. Next thing Jack come up tell me something, asking money, and I said, 'Why don't you go ask money to your girlfriend? They got plenty money, you been living in the pub.' And I tell him, 'You not allowed to be in this house no more. You just go, keep going now.' And he took off. He was living at One Mile Windmill then — people go camp there. Never come back. Amy's daughter Gladys and her husband David Walker, they had a house in Sherlock Street. They bring him back there, keep him there for a while, and they come and tell us, 'Dad there now, staying with us.' Amy never went follow Jack, she follow me wherever I'm going! She been living with me from we kick him out, 1970.

Got to learn about own language, too

I was worrying about if we going to let them kids stay in the hostel, well, they might be go away from the mother and the culture belong to them. So when we get the house in town, I get all my kids from the hostel back to me now, so we can teach them both way. They go whitefella way in the school; when they come back home they still got to learn about the culture thing, or whatever food — bush food and things like that.

I was telling my husband, 'If we let them kids to go stay in the hostel all the time, it's no good for them kids. They're going to be lost.' Like these kids been in the mission, you know; they don't know their language, and they don't know bush way. They finish. We must be get them kids back to home and so we can teach them Aborigine way, culture and everything, and take them out bush on the weekend. More better for them. They learn about school all right, and whitefella language, and got to learn about own language too.

This other lot here now: no Ngarluma language, no Kurrama language here. Only my language and Yindjibarndi language. They looking for one now, but too late; no one using that language no more. That's what they're fighting here now. But it's too late — all the old people's gone. That why I didn't wanted my kids to do that.

My husband was still mustering, but me and Amy, we settled down here in town now, and we got all the kids back to us then, when we got a house, because we had six kids in the hostel. And they was doing good too. They never hide away from school, they was still going to school till they finish.

When I came to town, 1969, all my kids used to be

scared still. Policeman, and all the whitefellas; all the good ladies and good whitefellas, they used to be scared about them still. They go to school, they only good for the teachers, not for any other whitefella. We used to give them money to go to the cafe used to be there, and they used to say, 'No, we don't want to go — too many whitefellas there. We got to come back home to have lunch.' When they finished school they come back, put all the books back in the house, go down the river now, bird shooting. Shooting all the birds with the shanghai, and cook it there. They eat all the birds now! They used to be funny. Sit down there all afternoon in the river, come back here about six o'clock back home. They used to be scared, my mob. We used to tell them story, you know, early days what happened our family from the policeman and the Welfare. They still got that when we living in town. They never used to go anywhere.

The people in the Reserve don't like half-caste people

We had a rubbish tip not far from where the little swimming pool is now. The kids used to go there, and them kids used to come from the Reserve and get cheeky to them, and Charlie went mad then. He had a shanghai, he chase that boy, won't let him to go back to the Reserve. He was this side and that boy was in here. And that boy screaming, running this side and Charlie this side travelling; don't let him to come up to the Reserve. And they chase one another right up in that hill this side of Five Mile, won't let him to come to the mum. And after, he come round the racecourse now, that little boy — Brigid Warrie's little boy. And when they come to the racecourse, they was chasing one another like that, and he managed to get to the mother. When the mum come, Charlie was really mad, and when the mum come growl at him, he threw the rock from the shanghai to the mum now! When he come back, he was tired, and I said, 'What happened?' 'Now, them kids from the Reserve, they always get cheeky to us, and the mum come up tell me off, and I hit her!' Oh, he was cheeky! When we having a meeting in the school, she told me then. Own family too, because that's my niece, that Brigid Warrie. She said, 'I tell him off, when he chasing my son from the Reserve there. And he start throw a rock on me. He hit me in the back when I was going other way.'

They used to be fighting — the people in the Reserve don't like half-caste people. You know what, these half-caste people in Roebourne, they used to say, 'You don't go get mixed up with the Reserve.' They never used to go get mixed up, but my family, when they in the hostel, they used to go visit them with Mr Stevens. And these people used to tell them, 'Don't go meet them. They're black people there.' They used to say that, and that's why they used to do that to my family.

I never had trouble with the whitefellas or Aborigine people. Even Aborigine people, they got different language and I got different language. I just fit in good in Roebourne, because they know I help them. Even the white people come over ask help, you know, want me to do might be ironing one day. I go do the ironing or something for them. I used to do it. I don't say, 'Oh, you whitefella,' or anything like that. 'I can't do work for you.' I been like that all the time anyhow when I was in bush. Station used to want us to do something in the station for might be week, we used to help them. I never had trouble with people, you know. And now all my family never have trouble with the whitefellas. Even the Aborigine people, they like them. They fit in really good.

The kids knock off three o'clock from the school. One day Angus go to school; when he knock off he think about run away see the father now. His father working at Cooyapooya, where the dam is now. Angus had a little bike, and him and his friend run away. And when I come back from work, because I knock off three o'clock too, hello, this kid missing — what happened now? I could see his school things there, and one of the kids, I think Nina or Susan, tell me the boys they going in the pipeline. They trying to get to Cooyapooya. He was about seven years old then.

Anyway, we had an old Landrover, short-wheel one. I got in the Landrover and I took one of the boys, Amy's one, Kinsey* Smith. I took him, because I was frightened of when they're driving in the pipeline — that was busy road, bulldozer and everything working at Pannawonica now. And when I was drive the car, we could see the boys' track crossing all over — they was following the pipeline. They never went in the road, they was keep by the pipe. And it went over all the hills here, by the pipes. It was in the hot summer time then, and there's a square tank there; it's water in that thing, pipeline water leaking, you know. And they pull up there and had a drink and bath themselves, make them cool. Not long, too: you could see everything wet. We went past that river where Dekker had his camp just out of Woodbrook. Lot of whitefellas was there working. They went past that one, and a little run-through gate there now. We saying, 'Oh, they there now, they going faster now.' And they pull up. 'Oh, Mummy,' he said. 'Mummy.'

I jump out from the Landrover, I flog this one first — my one. He was screaming! And I tell him to put the bike in the car, and the other boy thought I not going to give him a hiding. I got him and give him a hiding — they was screaming! I had a little short stick. Screaming! And he put his bike in the Landrover and I bring them back then. And when the father come, I tell the father then — father tell him off too. Never hit him, just tell him off. It's dangerous — very busy road, you know — bulldozer, truck, water truck, everything was working there, and these kids was run away. Oh, he was really bad; I was worried, too. I thinking they going to get mushed up with a truck or some car. He think he just visit Dad, right up to Cooyapooya Station, that's long way. He go past one station and next one! There's a run-through there near old Woodbrook, just near the station there. They thought they was getting away, but I got the little Landrover! Oh, that was funny.

She teach us how to look after the house

That first house I had was the Boonas' old house, Alf and Sheila Boona. They the first one been separate there. They supposed to be buying that house really, but no money went, they just been drinking too much. And so they got kicked out, never been paying all the money for the house. Husband went back to Mardie and Karratha station, because they Martuthunira people, and Sheila Boona was camping at One Mile windmill. Now we got that house, and we was living there two years.

It was only three-bedroom house. My son and Dinah, they had spare room, and Amy had another one with her kids, and I had another one, and all the kids fit in there. No ceiling, just the old tin roof. No lining, nothing. He was hot! Really hot! We used to sleep outside all the time. Can't sleep inside, because the tin is really hot. That's the government people for you, when they first started treating Aborigine people. That's what they done. All the house in the Reserve used to be like that.

They had big mob of house in the Reserve, none of them with a ceiling inside. People used to build the boughshed — brush one, you know, leaf one. And used to put bags — you know, them chaff bag — all them things they used to put, to make it a little bit extra for the family. They used to cover one part of the verandah, and put a couple of bed there for the family. Not enough. And no good tree they had in the Reserve, only a couple of tamarisk, that's all. No gum tree or anything. And even the Aborigine people should have go and get them trees in the river, you know, to plant it themself, but they never used to do that. They used to have plenty of water, but they never used to make a vegie garden or anything. Most of the time they used to be gambling and things.

My daughter Eva used to help us. She used to get a bush kangaroo and things, bit of flour and things, whatever we need, you know. But we was good. I used to work in the Four Square shop every day. Do some cleaning, ironing and things, washing, and cleaning the shelf. Might be Monday or Tuesday I used to do washing and ironing, and then I used to clean the shelf inside the shop. Dust it all. Get a little bit of money for the food. Those days not much money, and cheap everything then, those days.

Old Gus Jager was there then, he's the boss. He was really good. He's the one show me all the history in that old Roebourne Gaol. He took me to that prison, and he show me where all the people been hanging, early days.

There was a big well there, but they buried that now, and they put a new building on the top.

'You see that new building there, Alice?'

'Yeah.'

'Well that's where the hanging place. They used to hang the white and black people in the early days.'

Gus Jager showed me that. I think about how the old people used to tell me all about that, hanging and shooting.

We had somebody look after us. Barbara Morris first teach us how to look after the house. She was a young lady got three kids her own, and they was fostering one little girl, and I used to look after them kids when she working. They just live across the road, and she used to help us with all the housing thing. Just the cleaning the house, cleaning the stove and things and how to keep the house. They used to get cooking gear too, second-hand one; saucepan and things. Mrs Morris used to help us with the shopping. Show all the price. We know the taps; we had a shower and things when I grow up in the station. Flushing toilet first time. Yeah, we had to know how to use it, and toilet roll and things.

It was easier in the station than town life. Town life you got to look after everything. In the bush, when everything cooked you have a rest. From cooking you got to wash the clothes in the pool of water — you got to go to the pool. But we used to manage out in the bush, because we brought up like that, see. When you got a house you got to do the cleaning the house first, then you think about start cooking then.

But we had all the furniture — table and chairs — somebody used to make it here. Tables and cupboards. And we had to get some more beds for the kids; them double ones, you know. We got that, so the four boys can fit in the one room. That was good. Summertime we used to sleep in the backyard. We never had a air-condition. Fans is going, and we had all the windows open sometime. Three family. Dinah had no kids anyway, she only young. Amy had four and I had six little ones. Yeah, that was a lot. We had a little bit of garden in the backyard, just few little things. Tomatoes, pumpkin and watermelon and rockmelon.

We used to pay rent. But I had no Supporting Mother or anything when me and my husband finish, only the Family Allowance, that's all. I used to go work for the money, keep the rent up and keep the food. I only get sixty dollar a week: hundred and twenty dollars a fortnight. Just enough to cover everything, get the bills and the food. Half-a-day job, Monday to Friday. I used to work in the shop, and Amy used to work in hostel.

We was well off

They moved me into the new house after that; 1972 we moved from Sherlock Street to Crawford Way. House too small — only three bedroom — and so they got this four-bedroom house, because I had my big son working for the Shire, and Dinah and them two, they married. We was good then. And new house, too, brand new one. They flash one — they got ceiling and everything inside. We was well off. All the kids was going good, till they finished school, till they do the apprentice.

Five of my kids been in schooling in Perth, high school: Marshall, Camis, Charlie, Nina and Susan. Susan come back early, when she was turned fifteen, and she had to do two years in Karratha then. When she turned seventeen she was finished; she was six months training then, in PWD [Public Works Department] office, see how she got to go, secretary, and she was doing good. Then she start work in the Shire, in Roebourne, when she was seventeen. Nina's worked six months in office in Karratha. She was doing the secretary job. When she finished there she come back work in the hostel then. And all my other lot of boys, they got the apprentice; Charlie and Camis, and Marshall was working out Meekatharra way with the drilling mob. And when he finish, he got a job in the prison then.

Nineteen seventy-six or '77 Amy start find a boyfriend

now! She start find a boyfriend, and she took off leave me behind! I only self in that big house now, with my kids. She took off to the village, and stay in the village with him. Never last long, because he's very rough, cruel man, and he nearly kill her. He jump in and broke all her ribs and her liver is little bit mushed up, and she was staying in the hospital for a while then. And from that she never look at him no more then. She thought she was better than me, going looking for another man, but find out this man no good.

I never find any more man soon as my husband finish. I know how to look after my kids. I can work, and I just live like that. I don't want to look for other man, because those days grog was full up in the village. Too much fighting. So I just said I'm not going to get married again, this will do for me now. Never had anybody no more from that time. I had big family to look after.

I used to drink, myself, but my kids used to be really sad when they see me drinking. They used to cry, and I stop myself. I can see my family upset all the time when I'm drinking. Nobody tell me to stop, my mind and feeling tell me I not allowed to drink because I got that children. I'm the one responsible for the kids; father's working. And that's why I just stop. I only just used to drink that big long bottle with beer, you know. Little bit cheaper that time, those big bottle. Three bottle every day I used to get. I never used to go to the pub; I used to get them when I knock off from work. That's when I get the grog and bring them home. 1969 I started drinking, then I just finished, because I think about work and kids there. They used to be sad, and I stop drinking then. 1977 I finish.

I was never smoking. Only one of my sons was smoking; because he used to live with Molly Hicks and all the Hicks family used to be drinking bad and smoking. He come up when he was sixteen to stay with them, you know, and that's who he got it from. And all the rest of them, eight of them, never used to smoke and drink.

I had no bank book; I never been in the Supporting Mother, I used to work. No money saved up, just whatever money we use for the rent and electricity and all them things. Lucky my son was working for the Shire, oldest one, and Amy and Nina was working at the hostel. They help all the bills. We pay sharing, you know. We used to share the money out.

But father used to give the kids money. He got to wait for the cattle to go in the truck first, because all he got to make money from them cattle. And when he used to get the tucker from Dalgety's, he used to share the food. He take some bush, and he leave some for the kids. That was good, when me and him back friend again now. We was good. But I tell him, 'Twelve months before you come back and see the kids, and I let you to have the kids.' Then he used to take the kids out, school holiday time. He used to take them out bush then, and I let him to come back and stay with us for couple of night or whatever is, you know, if he want to stay in town. He was good, then, me and him

Marshall and his wife Beth (second and third from the right) on their wedding day, 29 January 1977. Jack Smith is at the far left.

friend now, no more fighting, because of the family. But we never got back together again. He didn't wanted it, because he going with different, different women. Then he went back to Amy Gerald then. That's a proper wife, Amy Gerald; live with him for long time. She was good, too, looking after him. He got the stroke then, and when he got the stroke Amy was looking after him good.

Marshall, when he seventeen, he was working for a drilling mob around Kalgoorlie. And when he come back for his holiday he asked me, 'Mum, I got to leave you money, put money in the bank from me.' Because he know I have got no money. He start to bank. ANZ bank used to be here, and that's where Marshall put the money.

He opened the bank account, and every time when I get that Supporting Mother and Family Allowance, it all goes in the bank there. And that was good then, I was all right! I was glad, too, when I had that bank book, and saved bit of money for the kids.

Government want Aborigine people to vote too

Then one of the whitefellas tell us that we got to vote now, because the government people want Aborigine people to vote too, because we getting money from the government people and something like that. We find that hard for a while, you know. Somebody had to take us. Somebody took me and show us all the voting thing where you got to put a tick or whatever is. They got to come with us, and they got to show us which one I got to vote, first round, and second time, well we know how to vote then. We know who to pick, whether it's Labor or Liberal.

I think that's funny, whitefellas doing that. We never been voting for anybody out in the bush. The old people used to have a boss for the tribe, and he used to talk. Early in the morning, might be four o'clock, he let the people know what's going on this country. They used to talk — yap-yap in the morning. Might be some of the young people getting bad, well he got to talk a lot to all the relation family, what's going on about this young fellow or young lady, whatever is. And we got to have a meeting and sort something out with them people that doing a wrong thing. They start to talk four o'clock right up to six o'clock in the morning. That's what they used to do. Everybody still in bed. He just making a big noise! We could hear him yap-yap. We know, see, that man's doing everything good for the people. Let the people know what's going on. They used to be good, them old people, but you can't see it in this time. Nobody doing it now. We got no boss now.

I feel sorry for the children

When I come to Roebourne I had fifteen kids from other people, looking after! I had to look after them — they hungry and wandering round, poor things. Norman James the first one we had, when I was in the bush. Norman James, Thomas Cox, and David Cox, but I never count them, you know, because we was out in the bush. They used to live with us out in the bush.

I had five children my own, going to school here in Roebourne. And these people, children got no mum, they just come one at a time to my home. I had a big high house got four bedrooms. First one he come, and second one, and from that, little bit of time they're coming, you know; they know where the food and things, and the kids.

This lot good kids, and not drinking and things like that, my mob. They find out we good home.

And so I had a lot of them, and then two twins, Russell and Janice. They born 1970s in Hedland, and they find out something wrong with the chest. Because the mother drinking, she not allowed to bring them back here, so they send them straight from Hedland to Perth Hospital. They was in Princess Margaret for a while, then when they were six months old they come to Dampier; they was here for a little while. One of the lady from Tom Price fostered them when they was walking round, one years old. They went back to Perth then; that lady put them in Nullamarra Hostel then — it's a Aborigine hostel, I think. And the Welfare work it out, they want to send them back to the

family while they get used to the mum and dad. And they asked me, and I said, 'May as well bring them,' because the father belong to us — old Sandy. They was eight years old then, Janice and Russell, and they come up. Then I had them right up till they

Thomas Cox, 1996.

turned fifteen, and I tell them if they want to go see their mum and stay with the mum. Mother died when they was here. They was about thirteen years old, and when they turned fifteen they moved to the old father then. They was there, and after that I had the last one here, Emily.

I feel sorry for the children. It's bad when you see the kids. You know, when you see the kids walking quietly, it's hungry and it wants feed something. Them things. Yeah, and they dirty, running around. Andrew and Angus is good too, they never used to get cheeky to them, they used to look after them. We had one bed here, double in the one room, and four kids used to come, so they're full! I used to get just the Family Allowance for the kids, to help the food. But they used to eat what I served them; they take that and they only come back for more when school ended. We bringing a bag of flour, see, and make a damper for the children. It was good. We had couple of bread, but mostly the damper and the kangaroo meat stew, because the father used to work out in the bush and they bring the kangaroo meat home and keep them kids plenty of food!

I look after them to budget the money

I got a new job, then, Welfare job, because the people moved from the Reserve. 1976 they moved to village here, and 1977 I got the job in the Welfare, looking after them

Certificate
of
Appreciation

presented to

Alice Smith

in recognition of devoted service,

given to children in this State

of Western Australia.

President
Foster Care Association
of W.A. Inc.

date 18. 9. 89

Minister for
Community Services

Great mother honoured with award in Roebourne

BRINGING up nine children of your own is a major achievement in itself.

Bringing up a further 15 foster children is truly remarkable.

Yet that is the task that popular Roebourne resident Alice Smith has achieved.

Mrs Smith was recently rewarded for her incredible efforts when she was presented with a 10 year Certificate of Appreciation by Mal Giddings, acting supervisor of Roebourne Community Services.

Mrs Smith, who was born around 1928 at Rocklea Station, began her involvement with alternative care some 30 years ago when she supported a family for several years when the father was removed by authorities to the Derby Leprosarium.

First Involvement

In 1968 she moved to Roebourne and commenced country urban living and undertook her first involvement with departmental fostering in 1973, when a child, unable to reconcile to hostel life, was placed with her.

In 1975, Mrs Smith temporarily worked as a cleaner at the Community Welfare office and shortly afterwards was invited to become the first aboriginal voluntary assistant to be appointed at Roebourne.

These volunteers became known as "homemakers" and they are now presently titled, 'family resource workers.'

Alice Smith's child care commitment has not yet ended. She provides full-time care to two girls, aged four and 13, whilst being grandmother to nine families.

Generous Nature

In her role as "homemaker", Mrs Smith "trained" informally, the new social workers and officers when they arrived green and keen from the city, while she has also helped set up a school lunch programme for local children.

On making his presentation to Mrs Smith, Mr Giddings said the certificate was a very small token of recognition of her generous nature and devoted service to children of the Pilbara.

"Alice's reward for her commitment is her place in the hearts of so many of her now adult family of her own and fostered children," he added.

now. They were looking for somebody, and someone tell them, 'Best to get Alice Smith, and the people who non-drinkers, you know.' Welfare come up and ask me. I was a Homemaker; I'm doing the same job like Barbara Morris before with me. Everybody got the pension then — I got the pension too, you know, the Supporting Mother. The Welfare asked me whether I going to stop that Supporting Mother money, and I said, 'No, I got family. I going to get half Supporting Mother and half the Welfare pay.' I was getting half-and-half. If I'm sick, well my kids still have money then — Supporting Mother, see. I was working out like that, because the father haven't got money. He only got to do all the cattle mustering and do the contract before he can get money. I had to ask the Welfare whether I can work it out with little bit from the Supporting Mother, little bit from the Welfare.

Rosie, Tootsie and me, and Pansy, we four was working, and everything was working good, too. All the people got the pension, and I look after them to budget the money to different bills, you know. To pay the rent, and light and the water, all them things, and a bit for the shop, whatever they owing in the shop. Share the money out and little bit of money in their pocket then. Every pension day and Child Endowment day we used to do that. Tell them how to budget their money and things, how to send the children to school.

We had a big building in the village there, government one, and I asked the Welfare could we get a stove and

Dora Gilba, Doris Butler and Alice Smith, 1980s.

things put in there, and the freezer and the fridge, so we could get the mums to cook lunch every day, Monday to Friday. Because every time kids going to school, when they come back nobody home. They got to go to the pub and find the mums there, hang around there and all that. All the mums is drunk. We used to make the mum do cooking there before they go to the pub, and get their kids to come back to the Centre to have lunch, and we used to take them right back to the school. If they go to town they don't come back to school, they'll be hungry, still hanging around waiting for the food, see. They look for something to eat. Everything was working good then. These people in the village was working good too. They used to be really good too, all the mums. They used to pay fifty cents for the lunch for every children.

I been working with the Welfare for eight years, till my

knee going. When the arthritis was start, then I just finish — '84. I been eight years working in the Welfare, and that's when I got a good bit of money then, and we was all right.

When I finish with the Welfare, these three young girls supposed to still want to do all the job. We had another centre near the old people pensioner home, and all the furniture there, everything there. We used to sell it to them, you know. People used to send them, second-hand one. If they want to buy it they can buy it for might be hundred dollar or fifty dollar or something like that. It used to be really good. And we used to have a little second-hand clothes store in the shop. They just make money for some things we got to buy for the house. We was working good. They had everything in the house when we was working. Fridge, and a freezer, and lounge and a table they had, chairs they had. Now you go round there this time, see nothing. Because people damaging, fighting all the time with the chairs and tables. Nothing there. And now this time you see all the children stray again, wandering around.

Roebourne went down, right down

Roebourne was really good before the mining time started. When the mining time started, that's when the free grog started. Same time with the people in Dampier — King Bay they used to call it — and those single person used to come from there. They had no cop in there when they first started. They used to come all the way to Roebourne. And the womans here, they used to be drinking with them, and they used to beat them womans up, take them down the halfway somewhere, drinking. When they had enough, they used to send them back walking, and they take off back to Dampier. And that was a sad one then. People used to get knocked down in the road, drunk, in the highway.

Dampier started first, and after 1967, I think, the Free Citizens start. Everybody allowed to go drink in the pub now, and that's the end of it. My husband had a Citizen Right — he only the one used to go and drink in the pub, and never used to bring the grog back home. They can drink there, and when they finish they go back home. And when the Free Citizen Rights start, everybody free at the pub, and that's the finish. And Roebourne went down, right down.

They settle down good when we was working Homemaker, and everybody was all right. Children was all right, everything was clean. We had the Centre in the village there. And we used to have a little kindy there for the little people about two and one years old, and we used to get Ellery Sandy to teach them kids when the mums cooking, and they got someone there to teach kindy. It was really good working.

In 1987, '88, everything just really drop — finish. That was the worst time then. No children going to school, just in the street. The mums never looking after the children no more, mums just doing all the drinking and smoking now. No jobs; all the men never had a job. Some of the men used to be working for Ieramugadu Group, but not the young people. The young people just used to be drinking. Only the middle-aged people, and couple of young people might be there, the couple of good people, you know, can understand that they want money. But not the people getting the grog. It used to be really bad, no job. And Ieramugadu can't take a lot of people, you know, they only got to take so much, that's all. That's all the job they had, only Ieramugadu lawnmower job — they go to every town, mow the lawn — that's all they had. They only allowed to take four people in the lawnmower thing, mowing the lawn and the garden, and they only allowed eight or nine people going to Hamersley Iron from Ieramugadu. They can't take too many. Only three been working for Shire: Douglas, and my son, and David Walker.

Old days was best, in the station. Stations, everybody used to work. Women used to work man's job. A few people used to work in the house, and most of the men and women used to work out, doing fencing or doing mustering cattle or whatever they do. Something to do every day, see. When all the stations got rid of all the people, they all pile up in Roebourne — no job. Even the women, the girls, got no job. They finished, they lost. Last lot of people been in Croydon Station. Croydon was still going, see, and Mallina. Those people was working there. When that thing finish, everybody was pile up in here then. Different different group, lot of different tribe language here. They all settled down together because the white man's way now. That's what they was saying: 'White man's law now, no more Aborigine.' White man want them to stay together, well that's it. They lost right out then.

And 1991, '92, that ganja started then, drug. They started somewhere else first, and this people find out from here, and they got the same one now. And that drug, we can't stop them no more. I don't know. That's in Roebourne too.

Kids from six, seven right up to eighteen, twenty. All the oldest one, too. People that smoking and things like that, they doing it too. You don't know who got it, but you got to see all them struggling after smoke. You don't know who to blame, you know? I put it through the Welfare once, when my first grand daughter jumping over the fence here. I want the Sergeant and the Child Welfare lady to go and find out from the back what they doing, whether they're flying a ganja or something else. When they went round there they got the different answer — keeping the side, you know. But you could see all the young people going there. All the kids from the village, all up here back. They're selling that ganja. My kids didn't have it. Those days, 1970s and '80s, no drug was running round then.

They didn't ask, they just go ahead

Sometimes I go back to Rocklea Station again. That big boughshed belong Walter Smith at Bellary, it was still standing when I had the kids, and next thing this railway line knocked all the stockyard and things down. Railway line went right through the old camp, because they never was thinking of talk to the Aborigine people where they got to put the railway line.

Those days, Hamersley Iron just went ahead; they think no Aborigine there now, they go ahead with the mining. That's what happened, and they find out the Aborigine people got important thing there. Too late, everything finished. Even Paraburdoo, where the mine they're digging, that's where the red paint belong to the old people. They used to get the red paint to put the boys through the Law. They damage that right up. But they don't know, they never been talk to the Aborigine people, proper ones been in that area. They just go ahead long as there's a mine, because Lang Hancock was doing it. Lang Hancock never had a talk to the Aborigine people, he just let the mine go ahead.

Even the cattle yard; when I went round Rocklea I see all the steel ones. Right on the cemetery, they put it, right on the cemetery — all the old lady been buried there, and they put the cattle yard right on top of the old ladies. They might took all the bones out from there too, when

Left to right: Mabel Paterson, Amy Smith, Peter Stevens,
Joyce Injie, Nellie Jones, Chubbie Jones, Nelson Hughes, Linda Doolah,
Jumbo Giggles, Gladys Bennett, Noel Bennett, Merru George,
Clarrie Smith, Tadgee Ireland, Paddy Smith.
Most of these people grew up on Rocklea Station.

they was digging. Oh, when I was first there, my finish! I was that temper up, and that worrying about the old people been buried there! All the people under there where the big yard's sitting, and that make us very sad. They should have seen all the boughsheds been there, you know! They didn't ask, they just go ahead.

Now these last lot of Hamersley Iron people, they find out that Aborigine people got a lot of important things there. They been living in that bush before the whitefellas. And they find out all that, and so they get us to talk, you know, ask. That was the proper good way to do it, eh?

And now we got something out of it, anyway, in that Hamersley Iron.

Too many meetings

Now I just got to go to the meetings, go to meetings, fix up. You know, lot of people doing all the telling lies and things like that, never tell the story. How the old people been in the station, I still picture it, you know. I can see it like a movie, how we used to work. Well, you've got to tell that truth. I can't make it up, my own stories, that's wrong. If I do that, all my family will be telling lies, then, that's what I don't like.

We went to meeting up here couple of weeks ago, all the old people — big men's come now. Peter Coppin, Teddy Allen, and all the people from Warralong and everywhere. In Yule River we had a meeting, telling everything about the young people. And Peter Coppin said, 'See this old lady?' — pointing out me. 'See this old lady? This the lady that very sensible lady. She speaks in particular way for the people, she don't speak only things bad, or anything like that. She talk to the people properly.' Because in 1995 we went to the Elders Commission meeting in Perth. That's when they heard me talking to this government people; lot of big people was there, and I'm telling them what's going on all about the Aborigine people here.

'We got no help; no one helping us. Where we going to get help?' That's what I was talking in Perth, and that's what Peter Coppin reckons. 'This old lady can talk properly too, and that's the way I want you fellas to understand properly. No young people got to tell the old people what to do; you have to listen to the old people telling you. Because they know; they've been with the great-grandmother and grandmother and the mothers. They're the one got it first, before we. We only worry about money, making a story, that's all.' He was telling the people, nearly make them cry, people in there.

Peter Coppin, you know, when he starts, he talk like the old people used to be in where I come from. They used to get up six o'clock, old people. If anything going bad, he can see the young people going bad, well this one old man, he used to get up early, six o'clock in the morning, everybody in bed, and he used to talk to the people. Walk around and telling them what's wrong they're doing it, and what's not they're supposed to do. I can't hear anyone doing this now. All finished, everything — it's died. Only that old fella, Peter Coppin, I found out him there now, when we having the meeting.

I was at the College in Roebourne last year, but now I said, 'I don't want to go now.' They want me back there, to tell all the story and things, but I don't want to go. Too much. When you're worried with your pain, each time you've got something to do there. I been working ever since I come to Roebourne, right up to now. I been working all the time.

Now I tell my son I don't want too many meetings. Other lot can pick it up quick and leave me at home all the time now. I don't want to go to the meetings — too far to go driving, long way. We had to go halfway to Newman, last time, with the BHP mine people going to start the new mine. They're really good, them BHP mob; they want all the old people to tell them the truth. Even this Robe mob, about the railway line coming from West Angelas Mine; they took me there. They was good. They understand properly, you know, when the people talking. They don't want the young people to tell them all the rubbish word, they want to get it from the old people. They're learning better now.

APPENDICES

ALICE BILARI SMITH'S FAMILY TREE

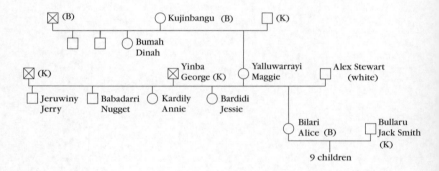

Squares represent males
Circles represent females
B = Banyjima
K = Kurrama
Y = Yinhawangka

They teach me I Banyjima woman

My grandmother, Kujinbangu, she had two sons and one daughter with her first husband. He was a Banyjima man from Mount Bruce. It's a old station: Birdibirdi, they called it, and whitefella name used to be Dignam. That's where the rangers' headquarters is now, and they changed the name to Karijini. My grandmother was the first one who crossed into Kurrama country, when she had all the little ones. She had her second husband there, Bindimayi, a Kurrama man, and my mother was born in Hamersley Station. My nana died in Hamersley Station; she buried there.

My mother was a full-blood Aborigine; Banyjima mother, Kurrama father. Her name was Yalluwarrayi, that's her Aborigine name, Yallu for short. Yalluwarri is the name of the windmill where she born. Maggie is her whitefella name; she had a whitefella name and Aborigine name. She was given away to her first husband — my nana give away that daughter, because that's the way we mix up; they frightened her own cousin-brother can marry her, or her own uncle or something like that. That's why they always give the daughter away to another tribe's family. Father and mum got to give away to the son-in-law.

My mum was a teenager, seventeen years old, and her first husband came and pick her up and take her where they was working in the old station, Bellary. He had a wife already, and he got this young girl, my mum, and take her there. Two wives, he had. This was long time ago. That's Kurrama country, there. She's the first Banyjima went there, married to the Kurrama man, her first husband. In Bellary she was helping; lining all the horses up, and driving the

211

spring-cart and things. She had no children then. That was in 1918, I think, somewhere about there.

Then she was pregnant with my oldest brother, and he born in Date Palm Spring, not far from Tom Price, on the Rocklea road. They called him Jeruwiny — that's the name of that place. It's the Aborigine name, but whitefella made it short: Jerry. My second brother was Babadarri — Baba, and Nugget was his whitefella name. And then the first sister: Kardily was her Aborigine name, whitefella name Annie. My mum had three children with that husband.

When my mum lose her husband, she married again with my stepfather, then, second time. They had a Aborigine tribe meeting in Coolawanyah, and when they come to the meeting Mum was pregnant. The first daughter for next father, she born there. Coolawanyah Station is called Bardirha — Aborigine name. So they call the baby Bardidi, and the boss on Coolawanyah Station give her the whitefella name, Jessie.

And I born in Rocklea. I'm the youngest in all the brothers and sisters — five in the family. None of them alive now; only me, the last one.

JACK SMITH'S FAMILY TREE

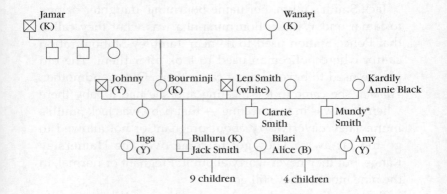

Squares represent males
Circles represent females
B = Banyjima
K = Kurrama
Y = Yinhawangka

All Jack Smith's family is Kurrama; that was their country

Jamar and Wanayi, that's the grandfather and grandmother belong to Jack Smith. All his family is Kurrama: grandmother and grandfather. They had two daughters and two sons before Rocklea Station come up; that was their country, they was there all the time.

Jack Smith's mum, her name Bourminji, daughter belong to Jamar and Wanayi. Bourminji-nha was what they called that Police Station used to be near Tambrey Station; ration camp, where policeman used to look after them. The old people used to have meeting camp there. Old grandmother, *Wanayi*, she came to the meeting and she had a baby there when they was in the meeting — that baby was Jack Smith's mum. They never worry about pregnant or not allowed to go too far away. They got to come over the Hamersley Range, but they never worry about it. Pregnant or normal, in the nine months they still go.

Bourminji came down to a meeting at White Quartz Spring in the bottom of Mount Brockman, and they found out that the policeman was coming to Hamersley Station, and they took off to the big mountain then, right up to the top. They don't want to go back to the station, they were not finished holiday yet. So the Yinhawangka old fella, Bourminji's husband, he leave his wife at the top of the mountain — she had the baby there then. They used to have a big spring on top of the hill, camping area. Not only that, a lot of wild honey that people couldn't get down here. A lot of food they could find in top of the hill. They could live there for long long time, if the policeman's around.

They leave the wives there when they know she's just about having the baby. Away from the policeman, away from the people. Only just a few womans got to stay there and a couple of man to get the food for them. That's the way Jack Smith born top of Brockman hill, and named Bulluru.

ALICE SMITH'S
NATIVE WELFARE DEPARTMENT FILE

Originals on Native Affairs File No. 381/36.

Inspector of Aborigines
To
Chief Protector of Aborigines

SUBJECT: Half Castes seen at Rocklea Station.

On my recent visit to Rocklea Station I saw some half caste children about whom I think something should be done.

At the pinkeye camp I saw two more half castes — females — Alice aged about 12 years or 13.

Alice's mother, I understand is dead. Both should be removed. Alice has not yet been 'married' in the broadest sense of the term and although mature should be brought away.

ALBERT P. DAVIS M/O
May, 1940.

ACTING D.C.N.A.

With reference to Dr. Davis' report at Page 24 re Half-caste children at Rocklea Station, I recommend that action be taken at once to remove these children to the Moore River Native Settlement.

Details are as follows:

ALICE   Female   12 to 13 years age
Mother   deceased (F.B.)
Father   Unknown

It will be necessary to communicate at once with the Onslow Police and arrange for the above children to be apprehended and brought into Onslow for transfer to Perth at a convenient date.

No doubt the Police will have to attend to this matter during the course of a patrol but delay should be avoided as far as possible.

A'g CLERK in CHARGE
28/5/40.
C/F.

Police Station,
Onslow.
22.1.41

The commissioner of Native Affairs,
  PERTH
Sir,

I am in receipt of your letter dated 15th January relative to
certain half caste children considered for transfer to M.R.N.S.

I was informed that all natives from that locality are now
on 'Pinkeye', and may be anywhere, so it would be a very
doubtful trip to take at this stage, and possibly until April
next, as it is not the working season and the natives will
possibly remain away for two or three months.

I am also informed, that, from past experience it would
not be advisable to make enquiries as to the whereabouts of
the natives from Rocklea station, particularly and therefore
from anywhere in that locality, as the natives concerned
would be informed of your intention and would go bush.

It appears to me that the only reasonable way of getting
these natives would be to make discreet enquiries and find
out definitely when they returned from their 'Pinkeye,' and
then make the trip with the chance of locating the ones
concerned, or finding out where they were on arrival at
Rocklea, and endeavouring to pick them up, if they were in
any accessible place, as I understand the country is very
rough, and they would not need to go many miles, to be out
of reach of vehicular traffic.

The mileage to Rocklea Station is approx. 230 miles from
Onslow so that the return trip would cost (… 6d. per mile) 11
pound 10 shillings that is if they were at Rocklea on arrival,
and it seems that that chance would have to be taken, for, if as
previously mentioned, enquiries were made, there would then

be a very remote chance of them being there, and hard to find.

As far as I know at present there will not be any patrols in that direction, but of course it may happen at any time that there will, in which case I shall certainly endeavour to locate. If, however you consider approving of mileage, it may be worked in with a patrol, and thus reduce the cost, assuming there is a patrol in that direction, and I do not have to make the full trip specially.

If you advise me of your views at an early date, I can keep the matter in hand, and if I should hear where they are situated, I could then go out. I certainly will not take on the trip indiscriminately. But you are probably more conversant with the cunning and movements of the natives than I, particularly if they have any idea that some of their kin are to be taken away.

Also will you please advise, in the event of the children being picked up, if I am to detain them here pending an opportunity of an escort South, and will you send one of your officers for the escort, or would the police be required to do it.

I ask this as you will possibly understand the infrequency of the State Boats at the present time, and it may be worked to fit the trip in with a boat, and save keeping them detained for a lengthy period, that is, of course, if possible.

(sgd.) J.C. Maller.
Const. 1506

3rd February, 1941.

Constable J.C. Maller,
Protector of Natives,
ONSLOW.

I acknowledge receipt of your letter of the 22nd ult., in reference to the half-caste children whom I desire to remove from Rocklea Station.

I agree that it would be better to defer this matter until such time as you feel reasonably sure that the children are at Rocklea and that you could secure them. I approve of any necessary mileage to enable the apprehension of these children but, as the funds of this Department are very limited and I cannot afford to waste money, I would very much appreciate your endeavouring to fit your trip to Rocklea in with the Police patrol, at the same time having some regard to the steamer schedule coming south in order to avoid any long period of maintenance at Onslow. I am anxious, however, to remove the children concerned from the unsatisfactory conditions that exist at Rocklea station and I now leave it to you to do the best you possibly can to ensure the removal of these children at the earliest convenient date.

COMMISSIONER OF NATIVE AFFAIRS.

The Commissioner of Native Affairs,
PERTH.

Dear Sir,

<u>Yours No. 381/36.</u>

I wish to advise that I left Onslow on Sunday 25th May
and travelled to Rocklea and other stations in an endeavour
to apprehend the children whom you wish to transfer to
M.R.N.S. and returned to Onslow on 28th May without result
covering a distance of 495 miles.

On about ... May I was advised by a man named Grimm,
who had been prospecting at Rocklea station, and who
rather complained of the way natives are treated at this
station, that all the Rocklea natives had returned, and in
obtaining a list of the names of the natives, the ones you
require were mentioned.

I kept the intended trip secretive, and Const. Mollings and
myself left at about 2–3 pm to avoid being noticed and word
being passed on that we had left.

On route to Rocklea I met an old prospector who had left
Rocklea a week before and he said there were no natives at
Rocklea but he was of opinion that they would be camped at
either an outcamp 25 miles from Rocklea or at what is
known as Stockyard Well, about 40 miles from Rocklea.

On arrival at Rocklea we found that there were only two
families there, and Mr. Walter Smith assured me that all the
other natives were camped somewhere on the Turee Creek
about 100 miles or more from Rocklea, and probably some

miles from any road and the exact location not known. I did not mention anything about transferring any of the children, and merely inquired of their general welfare.

Alice who is the daughter of Dinah is now married to a man named Bob about 45 years of age and is in the Pinkeye camp with the rest.

Smith informed me that some of these natives were at Rocklea about three weeks ago for rations, and it is doubtful when they will be in again, but when they are short of food and have dog scalps and kangaroo skins with which to purchase more food some of them will call, but not all of them. He further stated that there is no work for them to do at Rocklea, as owing to the shortage of feed, he will not be mustering until possibly about September next.

However, not relying on Mr. Smith's information went to the Outcamp above mentioned but there were no natives there, so I returned via Ashburton Downs Station.

I regret that I made such a futile trip in the main object, although it served to clear up other inquiries I have had on hand which I have reported on under separate cover.

However, now that I have seen the class of country around Rocklea, and the type of people to deal with, I would suggest, the best way would be to leave them and keep the matter in view and perhaps at a future date Constable Mollings may accidentally come across them when on general patrol or visiting that locality with the Service motor truck, and if so to detain them and get word to me.

Otherwise there is likely to be unlimited mileage wasted and there is no one who would give infinite information in that locality, and moreover these natives are more or less nomadic and rely on what wild dogs and kangaroos they can get to keep them in food, and consequently are practically all the time on the move and often miles from any road through the hills and bush.

I will keep the matter in hand and carry out inquiry as above suggested and make every endeavour to get these natives without further cost to your department if in any way possible.

I would be pleased of your advice in regard to the two girls Alice, who are now ... to be married. Can they still be taken from their husbands? I have passed the account for mileage ... through the treasury here for payment

(sgd.) J.C. Maller.
Const. 1506

19th June, 1941.

Constable J.C. Maller
Protector of Natives,
Onslow

I acknowledge the receipt of your report of the 2nd inst. In reference to your efforts to apprehend the children about Rocklea Station, viz., Alice.

I appreciate the difficulties and approve of the matter being held in abeyance until Constable Hollings is able to obtain definite evidence of the precise whereabouts of the children. In this event I am willing to incur a reasonable amount of mileage so long as I can be assured that the children can be secured; wherefore when something eventuates and you think it possible to apprehend the children I should be glad if you would telegraph me.

Alice is rather old and as she is now married to a native we might leave her where she is. This is a pity, but it is rather useless worrying about her at this late date. Had we known of her before, say when she was about 8 or 9 years old, it would have been possible to rescue her from the fate which has befallen her. It is now too late to do so, as no doubt she is now too far gone in native ways and … life to justify treatment at a native settlement.

I am not satisfied that Rocklea Station is cooperating with us in native matters. The station holds a permit to employ twelve natives. It was obtained at Roebourne. What do you think of Walter Smith's suitability to hold a permit? Do you think we would be justified in withholding his permit? We would need to have good grounds, and if you could assure me that he is acting contrary to our wishes I would look into the matter, and ask the Roebourne Police for a report.

COMMISSIONER OF NATIVE AFFAIRS.

Police Station,
Onslow.
30.6.41

Your ref. 381/36.

The Commissioner of Native Affairs,
Perth.

Dear Sir,

I am in receipt of yours as above dated 19th June inst. Relative to the apprehension of native children Alice at Rocklea Station.

I note your remarks as to the possible cooperation of Smith & Smith of Rocklea Station in native matters, and although I am not in a position at present to say that they do not assist us, I am definitely of opinion that they do everything possible to retard any progress or inquiry in regard to native affairs.

However, I intend taking another line of action to try and get these children, and will be shortly able to say definitely whether or not Smith is prepared to give any assistance, and will advise you of the result in due course.

(sgd.) J.C. MALLER
CONST. 1506

Two extracts — original on D.N.A. File 381/36

Commissioner of Native Affairs,
Perth.

<u>Re native matters Rocklea — File 381/36</u>

File no. 427/40 H/C Alice — this girl is now married to and residing with a half caste named Bullarroo, aged about 27 yrs, they are employed at Rocklea and occupy a hut of their own.

(Sgd) L. O'Neill.
Inspector.
19/7/44.

Bullarroo appears to be a very good type of half caste and was spotlessly clean and well dressed when I saw him. Alice also was clean and tidy and they appear happy and contented, there are no children of the marriage.

(Sgd) L. O'Neill.
Inspector.
18/7/44.

McB.PH.
427/40
6th September, 1944.

Mr. L. O'Neill
Inspector of Natives,
Broome.

I wish to acknowledge receipt of your report of the 18th July last which is in respect to the half caste girl Alice of Rocklea Station.

In view of your comments no further action will be taken for the removal of Alice, but nevertheless, I consider that this couple should arrange to be legally married as soon as possible. When you again visit Rocklea which will probably be in the early part of next year, I should be pleased if you would interview this couple and make known to them my wishes in this regard. You might also inform Messrs. Smith Bros. of my wishes.

D/COMMISSIONER OF NATIVE AFFAIRS

GLOSSARY

banaga	one of the Aboriginal skin colours.
bardi	witchetty grub (edible larva).
bijulu	yellow ochre paint for ceremonial decoration.
bilari	native tree with edible galls, *Acacia atkinsiana*.
billy	metal container to boil water in; 'boil the billy' — to make tea.
bob	slang for shilling in the old pre-decimal money.
boughshed	hut or shelter made out of branches and leaves.
Bourminki-nha	police ration camp near Tambrey Station.
burungu	one of the Aboriginal skin colours.
cocky	cockatoo or other bird of parrot family.
'cocky cage'	slang expression for police van which takes in offenders.
cyclone bed	a bed frame made of metal and wire.
echidna	spiny anteater, native mammal with long spines.
ganja	cannabis; sometimes used to mean any illegal drug.
garimarra	one of the Aboriginal skin colours.
gulimba	native 'tea-tree', leafy bush, *Melaleuca glomerata*.

gurlu	head lice.
jalyur	eagle feathers (used for ceremonial dances).
janjin	specially decorated dancing stick.
juna	spirit.
kakin	white ochre paint for ceremonial decoration.
kanayi	finish.
kargardi	hawk.
karla	fire.
karlajidu	black swan.
kartan*	corkwood tree, *Hakea suberea*.
karyardu*	child's maternal uncle who becomes a godfather.
killer	a sheep or bullock set aside for meat.
kubarru*	black paint for ceremonial decoration.
kukutarri*	native root vegetable *Clandrinia sp.*
Law	Aboriginal tribal rules.
maban	spiritual powers of 'clever' men in Aboriginal tribes.
mallalu	ceremony when boys become men.
mardarr	red ochre paint for ceremonial decoration.
marrimirri*	damper, a large round bread made with baking powder.
millangga	one of the Aboriginal skin colours.
mimi	uncle relationship.
Mingala	God, as recognised in Aboriginal belief.
Minbirridi, miggin	chicken-hawk.
minjariti	'Vicks bush', medicine plant *Stemodia glossa*.
mulga	native tree, *Acacia aneura*.
nganjali	forbidden food.

nyuba	marriage partner.
Paderangu	two stars which represent two boys in a story.
paperbark	native tree, *Melaleuca argentia*, whose bark peels off in layered sheets like paper.
purndut	male initiation ceremonies.
Reserve	area of ground put aside for Aboriginal people to live on.
rockhole	waterhole in rocky ground, rather than part of a stream.
shire	local government council.
skin colour	grouping determining who is entitled to marry whom.
snakewood	tree with twisting branches, prized for firewood, *Acacia xiphophylla*.
soak	hole dug near a watercourse, allowing water to seep into it and form a clean pool.
spring-cart	light cart with two wheels, drawn by a horse or camel.
straight	person permitted to be a marriage partner.
tucker	food.
waddy	wooden club, used for fighting.
walkyi	possum, native tree-climbing mammal.
wardiba*	men's secret song cycle associated with initiation.
witchdoctor	native healer (now considered a politically incorrect term).
witchetty grub	edible larva which lives in tree roots.
yandy	shallow wooden dish used for winnowing.
yumini	father relationship.

PHOTOGRAPHS

Pages 14, 28, 35, 91, 92 by Loreen Brehaut; page 101 courtesy Loreen Brehaut; page 17 courtesy Shire of Roebourne; page 21 Battye 649B; pages 6, 22, 27, 33, 39, 41, 48, 58, 86, 90, 91, 160, 193 by Anna Vitenbergs; pages 100, 106 courtesy Anna Vitenbergs; pages 25, 65, 120, 127, 149 courtesy Peter Joy Album, Goods Shed Museum, Onslow; page 96 courtesy Goods Shed Museum, Onslow; pages 98, 119, 141, 142, 190, 198 courtesy Smith family; page 204 courtesy Hamersley Iron.

NOTES AND CORRECTIONS

The Estate of Alice Bilari Smith advises the following corrections to the first edition (as at August 2014).

Pages 2 and 15: While Government records indicate that she was born in 1928, Alice always anecdotally maintained that she was born in 1923.

Pages 20 and 213: Spelling correction from 'Mundy' to 'Monty'.

Page 23: Name correction from 'Jimmy Edney' to 'Jack Edney'.

Page 24: Spelling correction from 'Ngaria' to 'Ngarla'.

Pages 27 and 28: Spelling correction from 'Buminha Spring' to 'Bumbanha Spring'.

Page 29: Correction from 'stockman' to 'stockwoman'.

Pages 36, 103 and 231: Spelling correction from 'kukutarri' to 'kukatharri' (bush yams).

Pages 44 and 231: Spelling correction from 'marrimirri' to 'martumirri'.

Page 62: Spelling correction from 'Moyen' to 'Moyet'.

Page 63: Correction from 'stockmen' to 'stockwomen'.

Pages 80 and 232: Spelling correction from 'wardiba' to 'wadirrba'.

Pages 90 and 231: Spelling correction from 'kubarru' to 'kubaru'.

Page 113 and 231: Spelling correction from 'kartan' to 'kartanya'.

Pages 115 and 231: Spelling correction from 'karyardu' to 'karjyardu'.

Page 144: Spelling correction from 'Thaianyji' to 'Thalanyji'.

Page 155: Name correction from 'Frank Dwyer' to 'Michael (Mike) Dwyer'.

Page 158: Year correction from '49' to '59'.

Page 158: The 'Welfare lady' mentioned was Mrs Rosa Rooney, who was actually the school teacher as mentioned on page 159.

Page 159: Correction from 'but we get used and used, now' to 'we get used to it now'.

Page 161: Correction from 'one old lady' to 'one old man' (refers to Mibben Low, a man).

Page 162: Date correction — only 1962 and 1963 (not 1961).

Page 162: Date correction — finished in 1963 (not 1964).

Page 162: Billy Dunn is a Warnmun man (not Nyiyaparli).

Page 162: Marshall came back speaking Warnmun (not Nyiyaparli).

Page 165: Marshall and Eva lived with Dave and Margaret Stevens in their house which was opposite the post office and not in a tin shack at the back of the Tsakalos garage across from the fire engine.

Page 169: Spelling correction from 'Allie Tucker' to 'Alec Tucker'.

Page 169: Jack Smith was doing the fence at the racecourse in Roebourne (not Hedland).

Page 181: Spelling correction from 'Kinsey' to 'Kenzie'.